3

GLOBAL POLITICAL STUDIES

KAZAKHSTAN

CONDITIONS, ISSUES AND U.S. RELATIONS

Global Political Studies

Additional books in this series can be found on Nova's website under the Series tab.

Additional E-books in this series can be found on Nova's website under the E-book tab.

Asian Political, Economic and Security Issues

Additional books in this series can be found on Nova's website under the Series tab.

Additional E-books in this series can be found on Nova's website under the E-book tab.

GLOBAL POLITICAL STUDIES

KAZAKHSTAN

CONDITIONS, ISSUES AND U.S. RELATIONS

RANDELL M. HOYT
AND
MORRIS B. WESTON
EDITORS

NOVINKA

New York

Library of Congress Cataloging-in-Publication Data

ISBN: 978-1-62948-356-6

Published by Nova Science Publishers, Inc. † New York

CONTENTS

PREFACE

This book examines recent developments and U.S. interests in Kazakhstan with a focus on human rights, international religious freedom and investment climate economics.

Chapter 1 – Kazakhstan is an important power in Central Asia by virtue of its geographic location, large territory, ample natural resources, and economic growth, but it faces ethnic, political, and other challenges to stability. Kazakhstan gained independence at the end of 1991 after the break-up of the former Soviet Union. Kazakhstan's president at the time, Nursultan Nazarbayev, was one of the top leaders of the former Soviet Union and was instrumental in forming the successor Commonwealth of Independent States. He has been reelected president of Kazakhstan several times and in June 2010 was proclaimed the "Leader of the Nation" with lifetime ruling responsibilities and privileges. Kazakhstan's economy is the strongest in Central Asia, buoyed by oil exports. Its progress in democratization and respect for human rights has been halting, according to most observers. Nonetheless, Kazakhstan's pledges to reform convinced the Organization for Security and Cooperation in Europe (OSCE) to select the country's leadership for its 2010 presidency.

According to the Obama Administration, the United States' strategic aim in Kazakhstan is to help the country develop into a stable, secure, and democratic country that embraces free market competition and rule of law, and is a respected regional leader. Cumulative U.S. aid budgeted for Kazakhstan in fiscal years 1992 through 2010 was $2.05 billion (all program and agency funds), with Kazakhstan ranking fifth in aid among the 12 Soviet successor states. A large part of U.S. aid has supported Comprehensive Threat Reduction (CTR) programs to prevent the proliferation of weapons of mass destruction. Budgeted aid for FY2011 was $17.6 million and was $19.3 million for

FY2012. Requested aid for FY2014 is $12.2 million (these latter amounts include foreign assistance listed in the Congressional Budget Justification for Foreign Operations, and exclude Defense and Energy Department funding; country data for FY2013 is not yet available). Among congressional actions, foreign operations appropriations since FY2003 have barred assistance to the government of Kazakhstan unless the Secretary of State determines and reports that Kazakhstan has significantly improved its human rights record. A waiver on national security grounds has been exercised in recent years.

Reportedly responding to a U.S. appeal, the Kazakh legislature in May 2003 approved sending military engineers to assist in coalition operations in Iraq. The 27 troops trained Iraqis in de-mining and water purification. They pulled out of Iraq in late 2008. Since 2009, Kazakhstan has permitted air and land transit for U.S. and NATO troops and equipment—as part of the Northern Distribution Network—to support stabilization operations in Afghanistan. In mid-May 2011, the Kazakh legislature demurred on sending some military officers to take part in noncombat missions in Afghanistan, citing popular opposition to sending such personnel to Afghanistan. In 2012, Kazakhstan agreed to facilitate the egress of troops and material from Afghanistan.

Chapter 2 – The Republic of Kazakhstan has a government system dominated by President Nursultan Nazarbayev and the ruling Nur Otan Party. The constitution concentrates power in the presidency. The president controls the legislature and the judiciary as well as regional and local governments. Changes or amendments to the constitution require presidential consent. The 2012 national elections for the Mazhilis (lower house of parliament) fell short of international standards, as did the 2011 presidential election in which President Nazarbayev received 95 percent of the vote. Some security forces reported to civilian authorities; intelligence services reported to an army general who was appointed as head of the Ministry of Internal Affairs.

The most significant human rights problems were severe limits on citizens' rights to change their government; restrictions on freedom of speech, press, assembly, religion, and association; and lack of an independent judiciary and due process, especially in dealing with pervasive corruption and law enforcement and judicial abuse.

Other reported abuses included: arbitrary or unlawful killings; military hazing that led to deaths; detainee and prisoner torture and other abuse; harsh and sometimes life-threatening prison conditions; arbitrary arrest and detention; infringements on citizens' privacy rights; restrictions on freedom of religion; prohibitive political party registration requirements; restrictions on the activities of nongovernmental organizations (NGOs); violence and discrimination against women; abuse of children; sex and labor trafficking; discrimination against persons with disabilities and ethnic minorities; societal discrimination against gay, lesbian, bisexual, and transgender (LGBT) persons and persons with HIV/AIDS; and child labor.

The government took modest steps to prosecute officials who committed abuses, especially in high-profile corruption cases; however, corruption was widespread and impunity existed, particularly for people with connections to government or law enforcement officials.

Chapter 3 – The constitution provides for religious freedom; however, other laws and policies restrict religious freedom and, in practice, the government generally enforced these restrictions. The government's respect for religious freedom did not change significantly during the year. The government generally respected the religious freedom of most registered religious groups; however, it enforced restrictions and harassed unregistered and minority religious groups, often through fines and raids. The government implemented a 2011 law applying stringent mandatory registration requirements on missionaries and religious groups. The law gives the government broad grounds to deny religious groups legal status. While most religious groups managed to obtain legal registration, some were denied registration because they lacked the requisite number of members, and a few groups, such as Scientologists, the Unification Church, and Ahmadi Muslims, were denied registration based on their religious beliefs. The Religious Affairs Agency's (RAA) very broad mandate provides the potential to restrict religious freedom further, and its rules seem to require all Muslim groups to register under the Hanafi Sunni Spiritual Administration of Muslims in Kazakhstan (SAMK).

There were reports of societal discrimination based on religious affiliation, belief, or practice. Muslim, Russian Orthodox, Roman Catholic, Lutheran, and Jewish leaders reported high levels of acceptance in society.

The ambassador and other U.S. officials engaged in extensive private and public dialogue with the government to urge that implementation of the 2011 law on religion be consistent with the country's constitutional provisions for religious freedom and with its international commitments.

Chapter 4 – Kazakhstan has made significant progress toward the creation of a market economy since it gained independence in 1991, and the European Union (2000) and the U.S. Department of Commerce (March 2002) have granted it market economy status. Kazakhstan also has attracted significant foreign investment since independence. As of September 30 2012, foreign investors had placed a total of $177.7 billion in Kazakhstan, primarily in the oil and gas sector. Kazakhstan is widely considered to have the best investment climate in the region. Numerous international firms have established regional headquarters in Kazakhstan.

The government's Program for Accelerated Industrial Development, part of its “Road Map for Business 2020,” created investment priorities aimed at diversifying Kazakhstan's economy away from an overdependence on extractive industries. The government of Kazakhstan adopted a "National Plan for Attracting Investment" in December 2011 which seeks to improve the investment climate by simplifying visa procedures, customs clearance, and transit across borders, as well as establishing special service centers for foreign investors under regional municipal authorities. In 2012, every regional government set up an Investors’ Service Center.

In 2011, Kazakhstan announced the goal of joining the Organization of Economic Cooperation and Development (OECD). To meet OECD requirements, the government will need to amend its investment legislation.

In: Kazakhstan ISBN: 978-1-62948-356-6
Editors: R. M. Hoyt and M. B. Weston © 2013 Nova Science Publishers, Inc.

Chapter 1

KAZAKHSTAN: RECENT DEVELOPMENTS AND U.S. INTERESTS*

Jim Nichol

SUMMARY

Kazakhstan is an important power in Central Asia by virtue of its geographic location, large territory, ample natural resources, and economic growth, but it faces ethnic, political, and other challenges to stability. Kazakhstan gained independence at the end of 1991 after the break-up of the former Soviet Union. Kazakhstan's president at the time, Nursultan Nazarbayev, was one of the top leaders of the former Soviet Union and was instrumental in forming the successor Commonwealth of Independent States. He has been reelected president of Kazakhstan several times and in June 2010 was proclaimed the "Leader of the Nation" with lifetime ruling responsibilities and privileges. Kazakhstan's economy is the strongest in Central Asia, buoyed by oil exports. Its progress in democratization and respect for human rights has been halting, according to most observers. Nonetheless, Kazakhstan's pledges to reform convinced the Organization for Security and Cooperation in Europe (OSCE) to select the country's leadership for its 2010 presidency.

According to the Obama Administration, the United States' strategic aim in Kazakhstan is to help the country develop into a stable, secure, and

* This is an edited, reformatted and augmented version of a Congressional Research Service publication, CRS Report for Congress 97-1058, prepared for Members and Committees of Congress, from www.crs.gov, dated July 22, 2013.

democratic country that embraces free market competition and rule of law, and is a respected regional leader. Cumulative U.S. aid budgeted for Kazakhstan in fiscal years 1992 through 2010 was $2.05 billion (all program and agency funds), with Kazakhstan ranking fifth in aid among the 12 Soviet successor states. A large part of U.S. aid has supported Comprehensive Threat Reduction (CTR) programs to prevent the proliferation of weapons of mass destruction. Budgeted aid for FY2011 was $17.6 million and was $19.3 million for FY2012. Requested aid for FY2014 is $12.2 million (these latter amounts include foreign assistance listed in the Congressional Budget Justification for Foreign Operations, and exclude Defense and Energy Department funding; country data for FY2013 is not yet available). Among congressional actions, foreign operations appropriations since FY2003 have barred assistance to the government of Kazakhstan unless the Secretary of State determines and reports that Kazakhstan has significantly improved its human rights record. A waiver on national security grounds has been exercised in recent years.

Reportedly responding to a U.S. appeal, the Kazakh legislature in May 2003 approved sending military engineers to assist in coalition operations in Iraq. The 27 troops trained Iraqis in de-mining and water purification. They pulled out of Iraq in late 2008. Since 2009, Kazakhstan has permitted air and land transit for U.S. and NATO troops and equipment—as part of the Northern Distribution Network—to support stabilization operations in Afghanistan. In mid-May 2011, the Kazakh legislature demurred on sending some military officers to take part in noncombat missions in Afghanistan, citing popular opposition to sending such personnel to Afghanistan. In 2012, Kazakhstan agreed to facilitate the egress of troops and material from Afghanistan.

POLITICAL BACKGROUND

Kazakhstan's moves toward democracy have been halting. The 1995 constitution establishes strong presidential power. As further fleshed out by a presidential edict, the legislature cannot control the budget, initiate constitutional changes, or exercise oversight over the executive branch. Most bills are initiated by the president, and if the legislature fails within 30 days to pass one of his "urgent" bills, he may issue it by decree. The bicameral legislature consists of a popularly elected lower chamber, the Majilis, and an upper chamber, the Senate, whose members are indirectly elected by regional assemblies or by the president. A People's Assembly composed of cultural and ethnic leaders serves as a presidential forum. A law in 2000 guaranteed the president certain post-retirement powers, as well as immunity from prosecution. These powers include the chairmanship of the People's Assembly and membership on the Security Council and Constitutional Council, and the right to advise the incumbent president and to retain a role in "initiatives on the country's development."

Kazakhstan: Basic Facts

Area and Population: Land area is 1,049,200 sq. mi.; about four times the size of Texas. The population is 17.74 million (*The World Factbook*, mid-2013 est.).

Ethnicity: 63.1% are Kazakh and 23.7% are Russian (2009 Kazakh census). Other ethnic groups include Uzbeks, Tatars, Uighurs, and Germans.

Gross Domestic Product: $235.6 billion; per capita GDP is about 14,100 (*The World Factbook*, 2012 est., purchasing power parity).

Political Leaders: President: Nursultan Nazarbayev; *Chair of the Majilis*: Nurlan Nigmatulin; *Chair of the Senate*: Kayrat Mami; *Prime Minister*: Serik Akhmetov; *Foreign Minister*: Yerlan Idrisov; *Defense Minister*: Adilbek Dzhaksybekov.

Biography: Nazarbayev, born in 1940, moved up through the ranks of the Kazakh Communist Party (KCP), becoming its head in 1989. He also was appointed president by the legislature in 1990. He resigned from the KCP in 1991 and won an unopposed popular election as president in December 1991. A 1995 referendum extended his rule. He was reelected in 1999, 2005, and 2011. In 2000, legislation granted him some official powers for life, and in 2007 he was exempted from term limits.

On December 4, 2005, President Nazarbayev was reelected with 91.1% of 6.74 million votes cast in a five-man race. Many observers credited economic growth in the country and increases in pensions and state wages as bolstering Nazarbayev's popularity. He campaigned widely and pledged democratic reforms and poverty relief. Five pro-government parties formed a People's Coalition to back him. Many oppositionists supported a Movement for a Just Kazakhstan, which backed Zharmakhan Tuyakbay, the head of the Social Democratic Party. Another candidate, Alikhan Baymenov, had been nominated by the "moderate opposition" Ak Zhol Party. Observers from the Organization for Security and Cooperation in Europe (OSCE) and others assessed the election as progressive but still falling short of a free and fair race.

The legislature approved constitutional changes in May 2007 that President Nazarbayev claimed would increase legislative power and boost democratization. The changes included increasing the number of deputies in both legislative chambers, decreasing the president's term in office from seven to five years (reversing a 1998 change from five to seven years), and requiring a court order in case of detention or arrest. Seemingly nonreformist changes included a requirement for a two-thirds vote in each legislative chamber to override presidential alterations to approved bills, a provision that nine deputies of the Majilis (the lower legislative chamber) are appointed by the People's Assembly, and a change "initiated" by the legislature excluding Nazarbayev from term limits. Visiting former U.S. Assistant Secretary of State Richard Boucher stated in June 2007 that "these constitutional amendments go in the right direction.... [and] point the way to a stable, democratic system."[1]

An early Majilis election was called for August 18, 2007. As per constitutional amendments and election law changes, the size of the chamber was increased to 107 members. Ninety-eight members were to be elected by party lists and nine by the People's Assembly headed by the president. Seven parties were registered for the election, six of which were pro-government and one of which was an opposition party, the National Social Democratic Party. The ruling party, Nur-Otan (Fatherland's Ray of Light), reportedly received 88.05% of 8.87 million votes cast and won all 98 seats. The other parties were unable to clear a 7% threshold needed to win seats. Observers from the OSCE praised some positive aspects of the vote, but judged it as falling short of a free and fair race.[2] In 2009, the Azat (Freedom) Party and the National Social Democratic Party announced that they were merging to increase their electoral prospects, but the government has refused to register the new party.

Legislation approved in May 2010 proclaimed Nazarbayev the "Leader of the Nation" ("*El Basy*") and reiterated and may have broadened lifetime powers granted in 2000 even if he retires from the presidency. The underlying purpose of the legislation may have been its guarantees of lifetime immunity from prosecution and other protections for the president and his family, including their business dealings. Nazarbayev refused to sign the bills into law, stating that although he was honored by the designation, he did not need such "puffery," and that his family should be covered by the same laws as everyone else. Despite these seeming protestations, he did not formally veto the bills, so under a law implementing the constitution,[3] they went into effect in mid-June 2010. He explained that he did not veto the bills because he was certain the legislature would bow to the wishes of the people and over-ride a veto.

The April 2011 Presidential Election

In late 2010, supporters of President Nazarbayev launched a petition drive to hold a referendum to approve extending his term in office until December 2020 (a similar referendum had been held in 1995 to extend his term to 1999). The United States and other countries and international organizations were critical of the proposed referendum. The Kazakh legislature quickly approved a bill to hold a referendum even before the petition drive was complete, but President Nazarbayev vetoed the legislation. The legislature overrode his veto (by this time, reportedly two-thirds of the electorate had signed the petition), but the Constitutional Council ruled at the end of January 2011 against the legitimacy of proposed constitutional changes necessary to hold the referendum. President Nazarbayev claimed that to gratify the petition-signers who had endorsed his presidency and to uphold democracy, he would move up the date of the next scheduled presidential election from late 2012 to April 3, 2011.

Many opposition politicians decried the holding of a sudden presidential election. They claimed that they would not be able to mount adequate campaigns in only a few weeks, while Nazarbayev's supporters had already mobilized to carry out the petition drive. During a three-week registration period, three candidates besides the president were able to satisfy the many requirements necessary to run (two of these also had run in the 2005 presidential election), while other more well-known opposition politicians refused to run, were unable to satisfy the various requirements, or were denied registration. All of the presidential candidates proclaimed that they wanted Nazarbayev to win, and one candidate announced on voting day that he had cast his ballot for the incumbent. The Kazakh Central Electoral Commission (CEC) reported that 89.99% of 9.3 million voters turned out and that Nazarbayev was reelected with 95.55% of the vote. According to OSCE monitors, "needed reforms for holding genuine democratic elections still have to materialize as this election revealed shortcomings similar to those" in previously monitored elections. The OSCE reported "serious irregularities" during voting, "including numerous instances of seemingly identical signatures on voter lists and cases of ballot box stuffing," and judged vote counting as even more problematic.[4] The U.S. Embassy congratulated

Nazarbayev on his reelection and "welcome[d] Kazakhstan's commitments to further liberalize the political environment and believe[d] that continued improvements in the electoral process are critical components."[5]

The January 2012 Legislative Election

For the third time during his period of rule, Kazakhstan's President Nazarbayev issued a decree on November 16, 2011, dismissing the legislature and setting early elections for January 15, 2012. He invoked his constitutional power to dissolve the legislature in case of a "political crisis" between the legislature and the executive branch of government. He argued that the crisis was linked to the possibility of another global economic downturn. His presidential advisor added that other reasons included rising terrorism and increasing popular discontent that would make it more difficult for the ruling party to win if the election were held at the normal time in late 2012.[6]

Of the 107 seats in the lower legislative chamber (the Majilis), 98 were to be allocated through party list voting, with the remaining 9 members selected by the Assembly of People of Kazakhstan. Critics complained that the holding of an early election appeared aimed—as in the case of the early presidential election—to hinder the political opposition from preparing for the election. Critics also alleged that the government had prepared for an early election, including by suspending the activities of the opposition Communist Party in October 2011, on the grounds that the party was trying to form an illegal alliance with an unregistered party to participate in a future legislative election. Another possible preparatory move included the Ak Zhal Party's selection of Azat Peruashev, who allegedly is a supporter of Nazarbayev, as its head. Under a law passed in 2009, more than one party must be represented in the legislature, so that even if only the ruling party gained enough votes to win seats under normal rules, a runner-up party would be granted at least two seats.

Seven parties were registered to run in the January 15, 2012, election to the Majilis. One other party, Rukhaniyat, was de-registered two weeks before the election, a procedure the OSCE stated appeared selective. Days before the election, over two dozen candidates were removed from the party lists by the Central Electoral Commission because of alleged inaccuracies in their documentation, a procedure deemed problematic by the OSCE.

The official campaign season opened on December 16, 2011, the same day that a peaceful protest by striking energy workers in the northern Kazakh town of Zhanaozen turned violent, resulting in over a dozen deaths and dozens of injuries. Martial law was declared in the town and was extended to the end of January 2012, but voting on election day went ahead. Rukhaniyat claimed that it was blocked from participating in the election because of its criticism of the security crackdown in Zhanaozen. The riots contributed to more emphasis in the campaign to the need for boosting social programs. According to some reports, the government waited until after the election to launch arrests of many alleged protesters.

According to the final results issued by the CEC, the ruling Nur Otun Party received 80.99% of 7.02 million votes cast and won 83 seats, Ak Zhol received 7.47% of the vote and 8 seats, and Communist People's Party received 7.19% and 7 seats. The other four parties—the National Social Democratic Azat, Auyl, Patriots, and Adilet—failed to clear the 7% vote hurdle and won no seats. Even the presidential administration has stated that both of the minor parties that entered the Majilis are pro-Nazarbayev parties.

OSCE election monitors judged that the election did not meet fundamental principles of democratic elections. They reported that the legal framework for holding democratic elections was inadequate, only selected parties were permitted to run, voters had no assurance of which candidates on the winning lists might end up with seats, the open exchange of views during the campaign was restricted, and there were "significant irregularities" on voting day, including ballot box stuffing and "significant changes" by higher electoral bodies to vote totals reported at the precinct level. The OSCE monitors also raised concerns that the CEC had declared the winners before the appeal process period was over.[7] In early March 2012, President Nazarbayev criticized some unnamed countries in the OSCE for using election monitoring to "pressure" other OSCE members, and threatened that Kazakhstan and other CIS members might cease inviting the OSCE to monitor elections.

Post-Election Developments

Even before the election was over, observers reported that government arrests and harassment of journalists and opposition party politicians were increasing. In late January 2012, one prominent opposition newspaper editor was arrested on charges that were two years old, and Vladimir Kozlov, the head of the unregistered Alga Party, was arrested on charges of inciting social disorder in Zhanaozen. In mid-March 2012, the European Parliament approved a resolution that expressed indignation for the incarceration of opposition politicians and journalists since the election on political grounds and called for their release. The resolution urged the Kazakh government to reverse the recent further deterioration of human rights by undertaking reforms to ensure future pluralistic elections, to safeguard a free press, and to permit NGOs to operate freely. The resolution also "strongly condemn[ed] the violent crackdown by the police against demonstrators in Zhanaozen," and called for an independent and credible investigation of the incident.[8] On April 19, 2012, journalist Lukpan Akhmedyarov was attacked and wounded in western Kazakhstan. He has alleged that the attackers are linked to local officials. In mid-August 2012, Assistant Secretary Blake praised the January legislative election as marking progress in the creation of a "multi-party democracy," but raised hopes that the then-pending trial of Alga Party leader Kozlov would be fair, impartial, and open, and not jeopardize this democratization progress.[9]

In October 2012, several Kazakh human rights activists and others issued an appeal for the U.S. government to deny entrance visas to over three dozen Kazakh officials involved in the Zhanaozen violence, including President Nazarbayev. The Kazakh Consulate General in New York denounced the appeal, stating that officials and others involved in the Zhanaozen violence duly had been tried and found guilty in proceedings that were transparent and followed the rule of law.[10]

In November 2012, an appeals court upheld the 7.5 year prison sentence handed down in October to the head of the unregistered Alga opposition party, Vladimir Kozlov, convicted on charges that he organized the Zhanaozen riots as part of a coup attempt against Nazarbayev. The U.S. Ambassador to the Permanent Council of the OSCE, Ian Kelly, raised concerns that the case was used to silence a leading oppositionist and stated that the irregularities of the trial "casts serious doubts on [Kazakhstan's] respect for human rights, fundamental freedoms, and the rule of law." He also correctly predicted that the charge of "inciting social hatred" against Kozlov could be used to prosecute other oppositionists, civil society organizations, and members of the media.[11] On December 21, 2012, the Alga Party was banned as an extremist organization by the Almaty district court, silencing what one observer has characterized as the main opposition party in the country.[12]

In November 2012, the Kazakh General Prosecutor's Office recommended the closure of most opposition media on the grounds that they contained calls for the violent overthrow of the government and otherwise undermined national security. Courts quickly ruled that these media were "extremist," reportedly without substantial evidence, and ordered their closure. Reporters Without Borders has set up some Internet sites for several of the banned media.[13]

A new holiday was celebrated on December 1, 2012, entitled "Day of the First President," to celebrate President Nazarbayev's rule. Some commentators in Kazakhstan speculated that this holiday was established to further consolidate presidential power and quell dissenting views.[14]

In mid-December 2012, President Nazarbayev announced that most district and village executive heads (akims) would for the first time be elected in 2013, and that later regional governors might be elected.

In a television show aired in early July 2013, President Nazarbayev praised the past political succession in Russia—where then-President Boris Yeltsin appointed Vladimir Putin Prime Minister and then resigned, situating Putin as the acting president pending an election—as a "democratic" example that Kazakhstan could follow.

TERRORISM AND UNREST IN KAZAKHSTAN

Kazakhstan long argued that there were few terrorists within the country, but this stance began to change in late 2003 with the establishment of an Anti-Terrorist Center as part of the National Security Committee. Shocking many Kazakhs, it reported the apprehension in late 2004 of over a dozen members of the obscure Islamic Jihad Group/Union of Uzbekistan (reportedly an offshoot of the Islamic Movement of Uzbekistan). It alleged that the group had ties to Al Qaeda; had cells in Kyrgyzstan, Uzbekistan, and Russia; and had been involved in attacks in Uzbekistan. In mid-2006, authorities detained 15-30 members of the banned Hizb ut-Tahrir group. In April 2007, 16 alleged terrorists were arrested on charges of planning attacks against security and police forces. In February 2008, security forces arrested five members of an alleged Salafi Jihadi Jamaat, whose leader had received training in Syria. In September 2009, six alleged terrorists were sentenced to 12-17 years in prison for planning to attack foreign oil companies and non-Muslims. In late 2009, the Kazakh National Security Committee reported that the government had prevented four terrorist attacks in 2008 and three in 2009.

Several suicide bombings and other alleged terrorist attacks occurred in Kazakhstan in 2011, although the government appeared reluctant to release many details and trials of alleged terrorists were usually closed to outside observers. A suicide bombing took place in a security office on May 17, 2011, in the city of Aktoke, and a car bombing took place at another security office on May 24 in Astana. On the night of June 30, alleged terrorists killed three police officers in the village of Shubarshi in Aktobe Region. Apparently shaken by these and other bombings and terrorist attacks, President Nazarbayev directed changes to the law on religion that were duly approved in late September. On October 31, two explosions occurred in the city of Atyrau, one at the regional administration building and the other a suicide bombing in a residential area. A week after these bombings, two police officers were killed in Almaty by alleged terrorists. On November 12, in the town of Taraz, one person killed several police and attacked a security office. The same day, an attempted explosion reportedly was foiled and an attack on a roadblock was carried out in Taraz, resulting in additional police deaths. The Jund al-Khilafah (Soldiers of the Caliphate) claimed responsibility for the bombings in Atyrau and may have been involved in other incidents. Kazakhstan's Office of the Prosecutor-General claimed that Jund al-Khilafah was formed in mid-2011 by Kazakh citizens Renat Khabibuly, Orynbasarov Unasov, and Damir Nabiyev; was allied with the Taliban; was headquartered in Pakistan's tribal area; and was dedicated to "waging a jihad on the territory of Kazakhstan." At the end of November 2011, Kazakhstan banned Jund al-Khilafah as a terrorist organization.[15] Jund al-Khilafah also has claimed responsibility for attacks on U.S. forces in Afghanistan. In April 2012, 47 alleged members or accomplices of the Jund al-Khilafah were sentenced for the October 31 attacks.

On December 16, 2011, energy sector workers on strike since May 2011 and others reportedly extensively damaged and burned government and other buildings and clashed with police in the town of Zhanaozen, in the Mangistau Region of Kazakhstan, resulting in 16 deaths and dozens of injuries, the government reported. Some observers alleged that there were more casualties and that the riots were triggered or exacerbated by police firing on the demonstrators (video posted on the Internet appeared to back this claim). Protests and violence also spread to other areas of the region. President Nursultan Nazarbayev declared a state of emergency and curfew in the town on December 17 and sent military and security forces to the region. He claimed that the violence was pre-planned and financed, perhaps from abroad; that the rioters had been given alcohol and money; and that police had shot into the crowds only in self-defense. At the same time, he charged that local officials had not heeded the grievances of the striking oil workers and had given him misinformation. In response, he fired the head of Kazmunaigaz, the state-owned energy firm; ousted his son-in-law as head of the national fund that owned Kazmunaigaz; replaced the governor of the region; and pledged new employment and retraining for oil workers who had been fired during their long strike. Critics charged that he took these moves to protect his popularity and that of the ruling political party during an electoral campaign (see above). The government reported that dozens of individuals have been detained so far in connection with the protests.

A trial against 37 individuals charged with crimes associated with the Zhanaozen riot opened in late March 2012. The bulk of the defendants were striking workers and youths, who were accused of initiating the violence, although five police officers were being tried for abuses in quelling the unrest. In late April 2012, the Human Rights Watch NGO called for the trial to be suspended while an investigation of alleged torture and other abuses against those on trial is carried out. In June 2012, a court sentenced about one-half of the defendants to 3-7 years in prison and gave suspended sentences, pardons, or acquittals to the rest. Another trial of 12 suspects resulted in four being sentenced to 4-7 years and the others being acquitted, pardoned, or amnestied. Other arrests have occurred (see also below, "*Error! Reference source not found.*"). The Kazakh government has argued that it has convicted some police for excesses during the riot, disciplined some government officials, given unemployed workers new jobs, and otherwise admitted that it mishandled the labor strife in Zhanaozen.[16]

At a meeting with policemen on July 12, 2012, President Nazarbayev criticized them for not taking preventive measures against terrorism, and stated that "over 100 crimes connected with terrorism were committed in Kazakhstan in 2011-12. As a result, dozens of [terrorists and policemen] have died.... And we have to admit the fact that radical and extremist groups are putting enormous pressure on the government and society."[17] According to a Kazakh Security Council official, over 300 individuals have been convicted in Kazakhstan on charges of terrorism since 2005.[18]

In late July 2012, one policeman was killed and one wounded in Almaty, and the alleged assailants later engaged in a gun battle with security forces and most were killed. In mid-August 2012, a gun battle with alleged terrorists took place in Almaty, reportedly resulting in the deaths of several alleged terrorists and the capture of others. Authorities claimed that these terrorists were linked to an explosion at a house in a village near Almaty in July and to the killing of several individuals whose bodies were found in a park near Almaty. The terrorists were planning widespread operations, according to the authorities. In early September 2012, a bomb-maker blew himself up in Atyrau Region, leading police to engage in a gun battle with other members of the alleged group, killing five of them. In October 2012, three individuals were arrested in Uralsk Region on charges of sending funds abroad to support the Islamic Jihad Union. Some observers have warned that these recent incidents may have marked the revival of terrorist actions in Kazakhstan after several months of seeming quietude.

In November 2012, Nazarbayev called for tightening legislation to facilitate government efforts to combat terrorism, with the government explaining that the changes in law were necessitated by increasing radicalization of the population and growing terrorist incidents in the country. The bill was passed and signed into law in early January 2013. The changes included an apparently expansive definition of terrorism to include an "ideology of violence" and acts or threats aimed at influencing the government, including violence and "frightening people."[19]

In February 2013, the Kazakh National Security Committee reported that law and security forces had prevented 35 violent extremist actions and neutralized 42 extremist groups in 2011-2012. However, it also reported that it had failed to avert 18 extremist actions, including seven explosions.

In May 2013, six alleged terrorists were put on trial on charges of conspiring to commit robberies, to bomb civic sites and the National Security Committee building in Astana, and to assassinate senior officials. At the opening of the trial, the prosecutor alleged that they aimed to establish an Islamic caliphate in Kazakhstan.

Reportedly, Kazakh authorities are drafting a State Program on Counteracting Religious Extremism and Terrorism for 2013-2017, which some observers warn could further restrict the dissemination of religious literature and increase monitoring of religious groups, including through the installation of video surveillance cameras in places of worship and the monitoring of students studying religion abroad.[20]

In Congressional testimony in February 2013, Assistant Secretary Blake stated that "we do not assess that there is an imminent Islamist militant threat to Central Asian states." Nonetheless, he stated that the United States provides security assistance to the regional states to address transnational threats.[21]

HUMAN RIGHTS

According to Human Rights Watch, Kazakhstan's human rights record seriously deteriorated in 2012, in the wake of the violent clashes at the end of 2011 between police and demonstrators in Zhanaozen. Several of the hundreds of Zhanaozen detainees made credible and serious allegations of torture. Dozens of individuals were fined or sentenced to administrative arrest for participating in peaceful protests, a restrictive law on religious freedoms remained in force, and media remained under tight control amid attacks on independent journalists. A ban on strikes in certain sectors of the economy improperly restricts workers' rights.[22]

In its *Country Reports on Human Rights Practices for 2012*, the U.S. State Department did not report whether or not the Kazakh government's human rights record had improved during the year, but did identify ongoing problems and progress. The most significant problem areas included restrictions on freedom of speech, assembly, religion, association, and legal due process. Police allegedly tortured and abused detainees, often to obtain confessions. The government frequently arrested and detained opponents and critics, sometimes for minor infractions such as unsanctioned assembly. Lawyers and human rights monitors alleged that judges and prosecutors solicited bribes in exchange for favorable rulings in the majority of criminal cases. Lack of due process particularly was a problem in politically motivated trials. During the trial of Vladimir Kozlov, leader of the unregistered opposition political party Alga, authorities did not present evidence linking him to the charges of violence or the overthrow of the government under which he was convicted, according to the State Department. Although courts conducted jury trials for aggravated murder cases, observers noted that judges deliberated with the jurors and few acquittals occurred.

The government used a variety of means to control the media and limit freedom of expression, according to the State Department. The government owned 16% of the country's nearly 2,800 media outlets. Of these, most broadcast media were either government owned or allegedly controlled by members of the president's family or loyal associates. In addition, the government influenced privately owned newspapers and television stations through government subsidies. Judicial actions against journalists and media outlets, including civil and criminal libel suits filed by government officials, led to the suspension of media outlets and self-censorship. NGOs and monitors reported that such libel suits greatly increased in 2012. At the end of 2012, Almaty courts banned several opposition media outlets—including the newspapers Golos Respubliki, Vzglyad, the Respublika Web portal, and the Internet television stations K Plus and Stan TV—for allegedly "inciting social discord" and "calling for the overthrow of the constitutional order." The law on state secrets makes it a criminal offense to release information regarding the health, finances, or private life of the president, as well as economic information deemed "strategic." In September 2012, Minister of Culture and Information Darkhan Mynbai asserted that the ministry would ban unofficial reports or negative interpretations of official information during emergencies.

Despite these restrictions, some media criticism of government policies continued.

There were significant restrictions on freedom of association and assembly. The law defines national security threats to include unsanctioned public meetings, demonstrations, and strikes that upset social and political stability. Authorities seldom approved demonstration requests and used force to disrupt peaceful but unsanctioned demonstrations. An attempt by the Azat Party and the National Socialist Democratic Party (NSDP) to register as a joint party failed, with Azat losing its status as a registered political party. Violence against women and discrimination against non-ethnic Kazakhs in government, persons with disabilities, and those in the LGBT community were problems.[23]

According to the State Department's *International Religious Freedom Report*, the Kazakh government generally respected the religious freedom of most religious groups, but refused to register some minority religious groups and harassed them, often through fines and raids. The government implemented a 2011 religion law that provided broad grounds to deny religious groups legal status. While most religious groups managed to obtain legal registration, some were refused under various grounds, such as Scientologists, the Unification Church, and Ahmadi Muslims (see also below). The *Trafficking in Persons Report 2013* reported that Kazakhstan was a destination and, to a lesser extent, a source and transit country for persons subjected to sex trafficking and forced labor. The government did not fully comply with the minimum standards for the elimination of trafficking, but was making significant efforts to do so, so was designated a "Tier 2" country not subject to possible U.S. sanctions reserved for "Tier 3" abusers. The Kazakh government maintained some law enforcement efforts against human trafficking and continued to protect some victims and fund awareness campaigns. However, government officials were involved and complicit in trafficking, and the government failed to identify some potential victims.[24]

Seemingly indicating some of the problems of the judicial system, in late January 2013 the prosecutor-general reportedly complained to President Nazarbayev that several dozen individuals had been acquitted by judges, even though prosecutors had "proven" their guilt (seemingly equating the bringing of charges with the presumption of guilt). President Nazarbayev reportedly agreed that the acquittals were untoward and ordered the chairman of the Supreme Court to investigate whether corruption was involved in the acquittals.

In March 2013, a group of Kazakh NGOs issued a report that the government had largely failed to fulfill a National Human Rights Action Plan for 2009-2012 that it had drawn up in April 2009. The report stated that while a few recommendations had been implemented, the four-year period had witnessed reduced freedom of association, assembly, religion, speech, and political participation.[25]

On April 11, 2013, the U.S. head of mission to the OSCE Permanent Council, Ian Kelly, raised concerns that Kazakhstan's 2011 religious legislation restricts the rights of religious communities deemed non-traditional by the Kazakh government. In particular, he raised concerns that all Islamic communities were required to join the Sunni Hanafi Spiritual Administration of Muslims in Kazakhstan, and hold services in the Kazakh language, in order to gain legal registration.

Appearing to respond to this statement, President Nazarbayev stated on April 17, 2013, that "religious freedom is fully ensured."[26]

On April 18, 2013, the European Parliament approved a resolution decrying the deterioration of human rights in Kazakhstan since the Zhanaozen disturbance. The resolution "strongly criticized" court decisions to ban the Alga Party and independent media, urged the release of political prisoners, and called for easing restrictions on the registration and practice of religion. Seemingly responding to the debate on the resolution, President Nazarbayev stated that the "glass [of democracy in Kazakhstan] is half or three-quarters full," and that "democracy and freedom as practiced in the West ... are for us the final aim."[27]

On July 1, 2013, visiting British Prime Minister David Cameron stated in a press conference with President Nazarbayev that he had discussed human rights problems in Kazakhstan with the president, upon which Nazarbayev reportedly responded that "no one has the right to tell us how to live and to build our country.... I think that Kazakhstan ensures basic rights. We have open, free and alternative presidential elections, three political parties are in our parliament, we have working opposition, Kazakhstan has 3,300 mass media outlets, including foreign ones, and we do not have political repressions."

He also argued that building democracy and human rights was a long-term process that had taken hundreds of years in the United Kingdom.[28]

The U.S.-based NGO Amnesty International issued a report on July 11, 2013, criticizing high levels of torture and other ill-treatment of detainees and prisoners in recent years—including as a result of the detention of alleged rioters at Zhanaozen—and the lack of prosecutions of those responsible.[29]

Kazakhstan's Presidency of the OSCE

The 15th Ministerial Meeting of the OSCE in Madrid in late November 2007 decided that Kazakhstan would hold the OSCE chairmanship in 2010, the first post-Soviet, Eurasian, Muslim-majority country to host an OSCE summit. Kazakhstan's then-Foreign Minister Marat Tazhin pledged at the Ministerial Meeting that Kazakhstan would enact human rights reforms prior to assuming the chairmanship and that during the chairmanship, Kazakhstan would ensure that NGOs are able to participate in OSCE events and that ODIHR's mandate is preserved.[30] Addressing the Parliamentary Assembly of the OSCE in Astana in June 2008, President Nazarbayev stated that his country's preparations for holding the chairmanship included the elaboration of a blueprint he termed "the path to Europe," which envisaged Kazakhstan's integration into Europe in the areas of energy, transport, technology transfers, education, culture, and democratization.

Kazakhstan's progress in meeting these pledges was mixed at best, according to most observers. In early February 2009, President Nazarbayev approved changes to laws on the media, elections, and political parties. Political parties that did not gain at least 7% of votes cast in a Majilis election were accorded the right to participate in some legislative affairs; the number of signatures necessary for registering a party for a Majilis election was reduced from 50,000 to 40,000; and requirements for registering media were eased. Critics termed the changes minor.[31] One positive sign was an action by the constitutional court in February 2009 to strike down a proposed law that would have tightened restrictions on religious freedom (however, a restrictive religion law was passed in 2011). In April 2009, a national action plan on human rights for 2009- 2012 was drawn up and was presented to the OSCE. In July 2009, however, changes to the media law were signed into law that restricted access to the Internet and broadly banned media reporting that "interfere[s] with election campaigns," takes place during times when campaign news is not allowed, tries to influence election results, or influences participation in strikes. ODIHR had urged the legislature not to enact the changes.[32]

Kazakhstan assumed the chairmanship of the OSCE on January 1, 2010. It followed a varied agenda with emphasis on each of the military/security, democratic/human rights, and economic/environmental "dimensions" or "baskets" of activity of the OSCE. Kazakhstan stressed that it would emphasize several issues of concern to Kazakhstan, Central Asia, and Russia, among them bolstering nuclear disarmament; continuing the "Corfu Process" dialogue on the future of European security (including discussion of Russia's draft European Security Treaty); appointing a Special Representative of the OSCE Chairman to promote dialogue on protracted conflicts in the former Soviet Union; and supporting several initiatives regarding Afghanistan.

At an informal OSCE foreign ministerial meeting in Almaty (Kazakhstan's largest city) in July 2010, an agreement was reached to hold an OSCE heads of state and government summit on December 1-2, 2010, in Astana (Kazakhstan's capital), the first since the Istanbul summit in 1999. Kazakhstan had strongly urged holding this summit to "modernize" the activities of the OSCE. The United States earlier had raised concerns about the necessity of holding such a summit, but received assurances from Kazakhstan and others that a summit would address substantive issues of U.S. interest.[33] At a meeting of the OSCE Permanent Council (the main decision-making body; it convenes weekly in Vienna) on November 15, 2010, Kazakh Foreign Minister and OSCE Chairman-in-Office Kanat Saudabayev called for the upcoming summit agenda to include enhancing the OSCE's efforts in Afghanistan; bolstering early warning and conflict prevention mechanisms; reaffirming the rule of law and the role of civil society; promoting cooperation among international security organizations; and formulating an action plan to update the 1999 Vienna Document (provisions for confidence and security-building, including the exchange and verification of information on armed forces, defense policies, and military activities).[34]

During three Review Conference meetings to prepare the agenda for the summit, the United States stressed that in addition to the measures mentioned by Saudabayev, the agenda should include reestablishing an OSCE Mission in Georgia; empowering ODIHR to better monitor elections; and strengthening the powers of the OSCE Representative on Freedom of the Media, among other measures. At the same time, the United States reiterated that it did not see the need for new treaties or institutions to safeguard European security as urged by Russia.[35] The United States also criticized Kazakhstan's efforts to exclude some civil society representatives from the September 30-October 8, 2010, Review Conference held in Warsaw, Poland.[36]

According to many observers, the December 1-2, 2010, OSCE Summit accomplished a few of the goals set by Kazakhstan but fell short on most. Summit participants could not agree on an action plan, but issued the Astana Commemorative Declaration toward a Security Community. There appeared to be some progress in bolstering Afghanistan's security and development and in reaffirming the centrality of democracy and human rights as core principles. The United States and Russia clashed over the issue of Georgia's territorial integrity, including whether Russia had complied with ceasefire accords, and over Russia's failure to carry out its pledge to withdraw troops from Moldova. Lack of progress in resolving the Armenia-Azerbaijan conflict over the breakaway Nagorno Karabakh also was mentioned by the United States as a reason the summit could not agree on an action plan (however, a statement was issued calling for a settlement of the conflict). Although the summit declaration called for building on the so-called Corfu process to further European security cooperation, the United States and some other members of the OSCE had objected to Russia's call (supported by Kazakhstan) for a new European Security Treaty.

Economic Developments

Kazakhstan is the most economically developed of the former Soviet Central Asian republics. The country is a major regional exporter of oil, gas, and wheat. In 1997, President Nazarbayev launched a plan to create an economically developed, secure, healthy, and educated country by 2030 (see below, "Energy"). In late 2005, he called for bringing Kazakhstan into the ranks of the top 50 developed countries within 10 years. At the beginning of 2010, President Nazarbayev launched a five-year plan for industrial diversification in line with his goals for 2030, aimed at developing the transport, pharmaceutical, telecommunication, petrochemical, and food processing sectors of the economy. In May 2012, he called for developing transit infrastructure so that Kazakhstan would become the central hub of a new regional "silk road."

In December 2012, President Nazarbayev announced that the World Economic Forum, a NGO, had estimated that Kazakhstan was on the brink of becoming one of the top 50 developed countries, and reported that the main goals of his 2030 plan had been reached. He launched a plan for the country's development until 2050 to become one of the world's 30 most-developed countries. The plan emphasizes food, water, energy, and natural resources security, as well as education, training, and social support.[37]

In 2008, tightening credit contributed to the collapse of Kazakhstan's real estate market, but high oil prices in the first part of the year partly cushioned the decline in GDP. In November 2008, President Nazarbayev launched a concerted anti-crisis plan that included lowering tax rates and drawing $10 billion from a National Oil Fund (created in 2000 to stabilize the economy in the case of swings in world prices of oil, gas, and metals) to recapitalize banks that had nonperforming loans and large foreign debt payments; to support Kazakhstan's currency, the tenge; and otherwise to boost the economy. Declining oil revenues and foreign debt repayments led the central bank to devalue the tenge by 20% against the U.S. dollar in early 2009. According to the Economist Intelligence Unit (EIU), GDP expanded by only 1.2% in 2009, the slowest pace of growth since 1998.[38]

GDP growth rebounded in 2010-2011, but slowed to 4.9% in 2012, mostly reflecting declines in oil and agricultural output, the latter because of drought. Average annual inflation declined in 2012 to 5.1%. The Kazakh government boosted social spending and employment programs in 2012 following the labor-related violence in Zhanaozen (see above). According to the *CIA World Factbook*, about 56.9% of Kazakhstan's GDP in 2012 was derived from services, about 37.9% from energy and other industrial production, and 5.2% from agriculture, although the latter sector employed over one-fourth of the country's workforce. Although Kazakhstan's major exports are oil and gas, it also is the world's largest exporter of uranium.

The United States exported $882.5 million of goods to Kazakhstan and imported about $1.57 billion in 2012. U.S. exports have mostly been machinery and transport equipment, while imports have been oil, metals, and chemicals.[39] According to data reported by the National Bank of Kazakhstan in early 2013, the largest contributor of the $177.7 billion of FDI in Kazakhstan was the Netherlands, at $49 billion (which includes that by international firms operating through Dutch holding companies), followed by the United Kingdom, at $24.7 billion, China, at $18.2 billion, and the United States, at $17.9 billion. Most of the U.S. and other FDI historically has been in the oil and gas and mining sectors.[40]Among the U.S. businesses operating in the country (for energy firms, see below), Boeing has sold aircraft, a GE-Kazakh joint venture manufactures locomotives, and FedEx operates a shipping center in Almaty.

In mid-2013, the International Monetary Fund (IMF) conducted a review of Kazakhstan's economy, and called for the country to bolster bank supervision and extend tax exemptions for banks and buyers of distressed debt. It called for the National Bank to elaborate on the factors guiding interest rate and exchange rate intervention decisions, and suggested that there may be scope to allow greater exchange rate flexibility. The IMF mission recommended against further budget cuts in 2013 to make up for a possible revenue shortfall, instead calling for addressing such a shortfall in next year's budget. The mission advised that in order to diversify the economy, the role of the state must be reduced while efforts are taken to bolster human capital and institutions. The state should enhance the transparency of all government programs implemented through quasi-fiscal institutions, and private public partnerships as well as through the general government budget. The IMF estimated that GDP growth will continue to be moderate in 2013—at around 5%— in part due to weakness in the mining and metallurgy sector, partly related to a decline in foreign investment in the sector.[41]

The World Bank and others have reported that Kazakhstan has improved its business climate in recent years in line with its development goals, but that much further progress is needed to reduce corruption, revamp labor laws and business regulations, and improve the rule of law.[42] Kazakhstan hopes to complete lengthy bilateral negotiations with trading partners that will clear the way for it to win approval by the World Trade Organization by the end of 2013 for joining the organization in 2014. In June 2013, the EU announced that it had reached agreement with Kazakhstan on bilateral conditions for the latter's admission into the WTO.

Energy

According to British Petroleum, Kazakhstan possesses 30 billion barrels of proven oil reserves (about 2% of world reserves) and 45.7 trillion cubic feet of proven gas reserves (less than 1% of world reserves).[43] There are five major onshore oil fields—Tengiz, Karachaganak, Aktobe, Mangistau, and Uzen— which account for about half of the proven reserves. There are two major offshore oil fields in Kazakhstan's sector of the Caspian Sea—Kashagan and Kurmangazy— which are estimated to contain at least 14 billion barrels of recoverable reserves.

Nazarbayev's development goals for Kazakhstan rely heavily on increases in oil and gas production and exports, which account for a significant share of government revenues and GDP growth. The government has anticipated growing revenues in particular from expanding production at the Tengiz, Karachaganak, and Kashagan oil fields. While production is increasing at the former two oil fields, the latter oil field has not yet produced oil. Development of the Kashagan oil field began soon after its discovery in 2000, but has faced numerous delays and cost overruns, attributable to the harsh offshore environment; the high pressure, depth, and sulfur content of the oil; reported management problems; and Kazakh government interference.

In July 2013, Kazakhstan exercised its right to influence the disposition of subsoil resources by directing the transfer of the United States' ConocoPhillips

8.4% stake in the Kashagan oilfield to the China National Petroleum Corporation (CNPC). ConocoPhillips had planned to sell the stake to India's Oil and Natural Gas Corporation. Other members of the North Caspian Operating Consortium developing the oil field currently include Italy's Eni energy firm, the Anglo-Dutch Shell, the United States' ExxonMobil, France's Total, and Kazakhstan's KazMunaiGaz (all with a 16.81% stake) as well as Japan's Inpex (7.56%).

Phase one experimental/industrial production of 180,000 bpd up to 370,000 bpd is now expected to begin by the end of 2013 or early 2014. The developmental cost of Phase one has risen to $46 billion. The anticipated difficulty and cost of further development of the oil field—which could result in second phase production up to 1.5 million bpd—have raised questions among the foreign consortium members about the timeline and feasibility of such efforts, and contributed to rising concerns by the Kazakh government that its hopes for rising revenues from the oil field might need to be revised.[44] In mid-2013, President Nazarbayev reshuffled some energy officials, perhaps marking dissatisfaction over additional production delays at Kashagan.

Some U.S. energy firms and other private foreign investors have become discouraged in recent years by harsher Kazakh government terms, taxes, and fines that some allege reflect corruption within the ruling elite, according to the State Department. It also reports that "foreign Investors report that local government officials regularly pressure them to provide social investments in order to achieve local political objectives."[45] In 2009, the Karachaganak Petroleum Operating (KPO) consortium (the main shareholder is British Gas, and U.S. Chevron is among other shareholders), which extracts oil and gas from the Karachaganak fields in northwest Kazakhstan, was faced with an effort by the Kazakh government to obtain 10% of the shares of the consortium. Facing resistance, the government imposed hundreds of millions of dollars in tax, environmental, and labor fines and oil export duties against KPO. Both the government and KPO appealed to international arbitration. In December 2011, KPO agreed to transfer 10% of its shares to the Kazakh government, basically gratis, and in exchange the government mostly lifted the fines and duties.[46]

Kazakhstan's main oil export route from the Tengiz oil field has been a 930-mile pipeline completed in 2001—owned by the Caspian Pipeline Consortium (CPC), in which Russian shareholders have a controlling interest—that carried 693,000 bpd of oil in 2009 from Kazakhstan to Russia's Black Sea port of Novorossiysk. Kazakhstan's other major oil export pipeline, from Atyrau to Samara, Russia, has a capacity of approximately 730,000 bpd.

See *Figure 1*. Lengthy Russian resistance to increasing the pumping capacity of the CPC pipeline and demands for higher transit and other fees, along with the necessity of offloading the oil into tankers at Novorossiysk to transit the clogged Turkish Straits, spurred Kazakh President Nazarbayev to sign a treaty with visiting Azerbaijani President Aliyev in June 2006 to barge Kazakh oil across the Caspian Sea to Baku to the BTC pipeline. Kazakhstan began shipping about 70,000 bpd of oil through the BTC pipeline at the end of October 2008. Another accord resulted from a visit by President Nazarbayev to Azerbaijan in September 2009 that provides that up to 500,000 bpd of oil from the Kashagan field may be barged across the Caspian to enter the BTC or the Baku-Supsa pipeline. When the volumes exceed 500,000 bpd, a trans-Caspian pipeline may be built.

Apparently to counter Kazakh's export plans via Azerbaijan, then-President Putin's May 2007 agreement with Nazarbayev (see above) envisaged boosting the capacity of the CPC pipeline. However, this project did not materialize in a timely fashion, so Kazakhstan proceeded to upgrade its Caspian Sea port facilities. Kazakhstan also barges some oil to Baku to ship by rail to Georgia's Black Sea oil terminal at Batumi, of which Kazakhstan became the sole owner in early 2008. Kazakhstan began barging oil from Batumi to the Romanian port of Constantsa in late 2008 for processing at two refineries it purchased. Some Kazakh oil arriving in Baku also could be transported through small pipelines to Georgia's Black Sea port of Supsa or to Russia's Black Sea port of Novorossiisk, although in the latter case Kazakhstan might be faced with high transit charges by Russia.[47]

In December 2010, the CPC approved a plan to upgrade the pumping capacity of the oil pipeline to 1.4 million bpd, with several phases of construction through 2015. The increased capacity will accommodate boosted production from the Tengiz and Karachaganak oil fields, as well as from anticipated development of the Kashagan and Filanovsky oil fields (the latter is owned by Russia). Construction reportedly has faced delays.

In addition to these oil export routes to Europe not controlled by Russia, in 2009 Kazakhstan and China completed an oil pipeline from Kazakhstan's port city of Atyrau to the Xinjiang region of China that initially carries 200,000 bpd to China. See *Figure 1*. Some Russian oil has been transported to China through this pipeline, the first Russian oil to be transported by pipeline to China.

Russia is the major purchaser of Kazakh gas through the Central Asia-Center gas pipeline network. According to British Petroleum (BP) data, Kazakhstan exported 422 bcf of gas to Russia in 2010.[48] Kazakhstan completed its sections of the Central Asia-China gas pipeline in 2009- 2010. At the end of October 2008, China and Kazakhstan signed a framework agreement on constructing a gas pipeline from Beyneu, north of the Aral Sea, eastward to Shymkent, where it will connect with the Central Asia-China gas pipeline. The pipeline is planned initially to supply 176.6 bcf to southern Kazakhstan and 176.6 bcf to China. Pipeline construction began in September 2011 and to be completed by 2015.

Kazakh officials have appeared to make contradictory statements about providing gas for European customers via a possible trans-Caspian pipeline traversing the South Caucasus and Turkey. President Nazarbayev appeared to support the possible transit of Kazakh gas through Turkey when he stated on October 22, 2009, during a visit to Turkey, that "Turkey ... will become a transit country. And if Kazakhstan's oil and gas are transported via this corridor then this will be advantageous to both Turkey and Kazakhstan."[49] Reacting to the decision of the European Commission to facilitate talks on building a trans-Caspian gas pipeline, Minister of Oil and Gas Sauat Mynabyev stated in early October 2011 that "we do not have available resources for the gas pipeline yet."[50]

FOREIGN POLICY AND DEFENSE

Nazarbayev has stated that the geographic location of Kazakhstan and its ethnic makeup dictate its "multi-vector orientation toward both West and East." He has pursued close ties with Turkey, trade links with Iran, and better relations with China, which many Kazakhs have traditionally viewed as a security threat. There are over 1 million ethnic Kazakhs in China, and 300,000 ethnic Uighurs of China residing in Kazakhstan, who have contributed to complicated relations between the two states.

While seeking to protect Kazakh independence, Nazarbayev has pursued close relations with Russia and other Commonwealth of Independent States (CIS) members for economic and security reasons. In 1998, Kazakhstan and Russia signed a friendship treaty; in 1998 and 2002, they signed accords settling Caspian seabed resource claims; and in 2005, they signed a border delineation agreement.

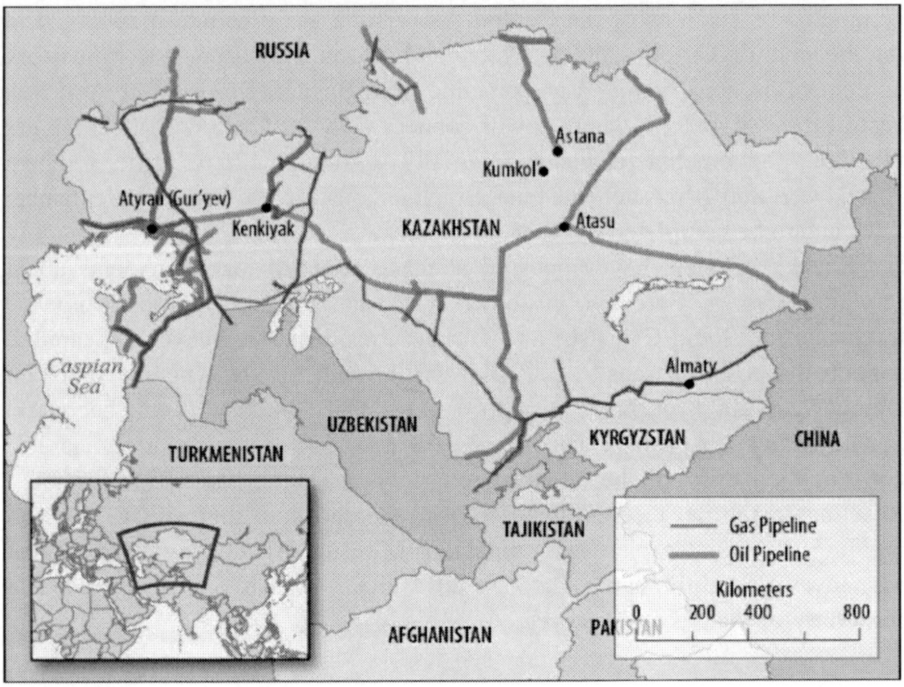

Source: CRS.

Figure 1. Map of Kazakhstan with Gas and Oil Pipelines.

In late 2005, the Central Asian Cooperation Organization merged with the Eurasian Economic Community (Eurasec; Russia and Kazakhstan belonged to both). Eurasec members Russia, Belarus, and Kazakhstan launched a Customs Union in July 2010. On April 4, 2011, just after his reelection, President Nazarbayev stated that "our foreign policy targets will remain as before. We have close relations with Russia and China, the EU, and the United States, and other states of the region are our big partners." In regard to the latter, he hailed increasing trade and other integration within the Customs Union.[51] Nazarbayev also has supported Russia's then-Prime Minister Putin's October 2011 proposal for deeper regional economic integration on the basis of the Customs Union to establish an Eurasian Union (which Putin stated was based on a concept advocated by Nazarbayev in 1994). Some in Kazakhstan have voiced concerns that Kazkhstan's sovereignty will be harmed by these integration efforts.

Kazakhstan's assertion of its national interests has contributed to recent tensions in Kazakhstan-Russia relations. These include President Nazarbayev's call for switching to the Latin script and for Kazakh and English to be more widely used;[52] his assertion that if Eurasian integration threatens Kazakhstan's sovereignty, the country will withdraw from "such a union";[53] and Kazakhstan's reappraisal of Russia's lease of the expansive Baikonur Cosmodrome space launch center and surrounding areas. In regard to the latter issue, a 1994 lease (extended in 2004) grants Russia a colonial-style concession over nearly 3,000 square miles of Kazakh territory until 2050 for a yearly payment of about $154 million. In late 2012, Kazakh officials raised the issue of renegotiating the lease agreement, and an inter-governmental commission was set up to discuss Kazakh concerns. In late March 2013, however, the deputy prime minister pledged Kazakhstan's "unconditional adherence" to the lease. Nonetheless, Kazakhstan has pressed for limiting some rocket launches deemed environmentally damaging.

Armed Forces

Kazakhstan still relies heavily on Russia for military training and equipment, but has expanded defense cooperation with other states. About 20,000 Kazakh troops serve in the army, 12,000 in the air force, and 3,000 in the navy. There are about 4,000 special forces, 9,000 border guards, 20,000 Internal Security (police) troops, and 2,500 presidential and government guards.[54] In 1999, Kazakhstan reaffirmed a CIS Collective Security Treaty (later formalized as the Collective Security Treaty Organization or CSTO) pledging the parties to provide military assistance in case of aggression against any one of them. Kazakhstan is also a member of the Shanghai Cooperation Organization (SCO), composed of Russia, China, and the Central Asian states (except Turkmenistan), which aims to combat terrorism and facilitate trade ties. In 1994, Kazakhstan joined NATO's Partnership for Peace (PFP) and regularly takes part in PFP exercises, but states that it does not aim to join the alliance.

A new military doctrine adopted in 2011 emphasizes internal threats to security, including terrorism and separatism; and intra-regional threats to security, including border and water supply disputes and political instability. The doctrine considers external threats such as terrorism emanating from Afghanistan as potent but slightly lesser threats. The doctrine appears to eschew security reliance on the CSTO or SCO. It calls for modernizing the armed forces and eventually creating volunteer armed forces.[55] According to some observers, the doctrine reflects the objective of creating the most powerful armed forces in Central Asia.

Reforms include the transition to a brigade-based organizational and staff structure, the creation of the Shokan Ualikhanov Cadet Corps school for noncommissioned officers, and other elements of a hierarchy of military educational institutions. In mid-2009, efforts were announced to boost declining salaries and other social support for troops. Defense Minister Adilbek Dzhaksybekov reported that he had completed reforming the high commands of the ground forces, air force, and navy in 2009 as part of the goal of creating a "small, mobile, truly combat-capable army." A new concept for military procurement calls for modernizing defense industries; purchasing foreign weaponry; seeking foreign technical assistance for upgrading existing equipment; and focusing more on command, control, and communications technologies. The Spassk Combat Training and Combat Use Center was opened in 2010 to train junior officers and to train all male civilians of draft age in military skills as part of a mobilization reserve.[56] The Zhanaozen violence may have spurred military procurement of added airlift capabilities and redeployment of some troops to southwestern Kazakhstan.

Kazakhstan reportedly has launched a program to bolster its Caspian Sea naval presence, including by signing accords with French and Spanish firms to obtain anti-ship missiles. In 2012, it launched a new domestically-built patrol boat. To increase airlift and mobility, the country purchased two C-295s from France's Airbus Military with delivery expected in 2013, and opened the Eurocopter Kazakhstan assembly facility in July 2012—a joint venture between the Dutch-registered EADS and Kazakhstan Engineering (a state-owned holding company)—to construct EC145 and EC645-T2 helicopters. Other military modernization initiatives include agreements with defense firms in Ukraine to build armored personnel carriers, in the United States to repair turboprop aircraft, in Turkey to manufacture optical and thermal sensors, and in Spain to build radars.[57]

Nuclear Non-Proliferation

After the Soviet breakup, Kazakhstan was on paper a major nuclear weapons power (in reality Russia controlled these weapons). All bombers and their air-launched cruise missiles were removed to Russia by late February 1994. On April 21, 1995, the last of about 1,040 nuclear warheads had been removed from the SS-18 missiles and transferred to Russia, and Kazakhstan announced that it was nuclear weapons-free. U.S. Comprehensive Threat Reduction (CTR) assistance was used for these efforts, and for subsequent control and elimination of nuclear materials and former chemical and biological warfare facilities. The U.S. Nuclear Risk Reduction Center works with Kazakhstan to facilitate verification and compliance with arms control and security agreements to enhance peace and prevent the proliferation of WMD. Among recent cooperation, ground was broken in March 2010 on a Central Laboratory to help secure Kazakhstan's collection of especially dangerous pathogens. Under the objective of combating weapons of mass destruction (which includes CTR and agency funding), U.S. assistance to Kazakhstan was over $1.0 billion from FY1992 through FY2010, which was about one-half of all U.S. assistance to the country.

President Obama met on April 11, 2010, with Kazakh President Nursultan Nazarbayev on the sidelines of the Nuclear Security Summit in Washington, DC. A joint statement reported that they "pledged to intensify bilateral cooperation to promote nuclear safety and nonproliferation, regional stability in Central Asia, economic prosperity, and universal values." President Obama encouraged Kazakhstan to fully implement its 2009-2012 National Human Rights Action Plan (but see above). President Nazarbayev agreed to facilitate U.S. military air flights along a new trans-polar route that transits Kazakhstan to Afghanistan, and President Obama praised Kazakh assistance to Afghanistan.[58] In March 2012, President Obama met with President Nazarbayev at the nuclear security summit in Seoul, South Korea, where President Obama hailed Kazakhstan's efforts to secure nuclear materials inherited from the former Soviet Union.[59]

U.S. POLICY

U.S. relations with Kazakhstan intensified after the September 11, 2001, terrorist attacks on the United States and U.S. and coalition forces began operations in Afghanistan. At first, the U.S. policy appeared focused more on ties with Uzbekistan, the centrally-located and most populous regional state, when a U.S. airbase was established. However, after Uzbekistan closed the airbase in mid-2005 in the wake of U.S. concerns about human rights abuses in that country, U.S. policy attention appeared to shift more to Kazakhstan as the most significant U.S. "partner" in the region.[60] Some observers argue that as Kazakhstan has developed economically in recent years, including by establishing closer energy and other ties with China, it has placed somewhat less priority on ties with the United States. These observers maintain that although future U.S. relations with Kazakhstan may not focus as much on security concerns, the country will remain significant to U.S. interests as a prominent economic and political power in the region.[61]

According to the Obama Administration's *Congressional Budget Justification for Foreign Operations*, the U.S. "strategic aim in Kazakhstan is to ensure and maintain the development of the country as a stable, secure, democratic, and prosperous partner that respects international standards and agreements, embraces free-market competition and the rule of law, and is a respected regional leader." The Administration avers that Kazakhstan has made significant progress—with U.S. support—over the period since it gained independence in late 1991 to reach these goals. For FY2014, U.S. government aid will focus on programs "that support Kazakhstan's evolution into a stronger partner ... that can play a greater role in promoting regional stability and economic integration."[62]

During President Nazarbayev's 1994 U.S. visit, he and then-President Clinton signed a Charter on Democratic Partnership, which recognized Kazakhstan's commitments to the rule of law, respect for human rights, and economic reform. During his December 2001 and September 2006 visits, Nazarbayev repeated these pledges in joint statements with then-President Bush. During the former visit, an accord to establish an Energy Partnership dialogue was signed to facilitate cooperation on nuclear, hydrocarbon, and electric power resources and various issues such as renewable energy and energy efficiency. At the 9th annual meeting in October 2012, an action plan for the next two years was promulgated dealing with these resources and issues.[63]

The Obama Administration launched annual bilateral consultations (ABC) on economic and political issues with Kazakhstan, with the first meeting taking place in Washington, DC, in March 2010, the second in Astana (Kazakhstan's capital) in late March 2011, and the third in Washington, DC, in February 2012. At this meeting, the United States reportedly agreed to work with Kazakhstan to attract U.S. companies and universities to establish a presence at the Innovative Technologies Park near Almaty. The State Department also announced that it was elevating relations with Kazakhstan to the level of a strategic partnership dialogue by transforming the ABC into a Strategic Partnership Commission (SPC).

The inaugural meeting of the SPC took place in April 2012 in Washington D.C. and established several working groups, including on non-proliferation and disarmament, economic cooperation, and science and technology. In addition, a "human dimension dialogue" involved a roundtable on civil and human rights held by various NGOs. [64] Apparently, these working groups are separate from other bilateral groups on nuclear material safeguards, on science and technology cooperation, and trade and investment that have been established by separate accords and which have held inaugural meetings in 2013.

No agreements reportedly were signed at the second SPC meeting in July 2013, also held in Washington, D.C., but the two sides (co-chaired on the U.S. side by Deputy Secretary of State William Burns and on the Kazakh side by Foreign Minister Idrisov) made several pledges, including U.S. pledges to continue to assist Kazakhstan to obtain WTO membership and to work to increase trade and investment.[65]

President Obama met with President Nazarbayev at nuclear security summits in April 2010 and March 2012 (see above). Also signaling the Obama Administration's interest in Kazakhstan, a Consulate General was opened in Almaty (the former capital and the business center)—the first such post in Central Asia—and the first consul general arrived in August 2010.

During an August 2012 visit to Kazakhstan, Assistant Secretary Blake stressed that "our relations with Kazakhstan ... are the deepest and broadest of all countries in Central Asia.... Kazakhstan is looking ... to play a larger role in the regional integration process and work a lot on some of the very important regional issues, such as non-proliferation and so on. All of these are very consistent with what we are trying to accomplish and [are] one of the reasons why we have a very good partnership with Kazakhstan."[66] In congressional testimony in July 2012, Assistant Secretary Blake highlighted growing U.S.-Kazakh trade relations, Kazakhstan's assistance to stabilization efforts in Afghanistan, and its global role in combating nuclear proliferation. At the same time, he stressed that the United States would continue to support the Kazakh government's further efforts to democratize and respect human rights. He reiterated U.S. concerns about the Kazakh government's use of deadly force in quelling unrest in Zhanaozen in late 2012 (see above) and about allegations that suspects had been tortured.[67]

Cumulative U.S. aid budgeted for Kazakhstan in fiscal years 1992 through 2010 was $2.05 billion (all-agency funding), with Kazakhstan ranking fifth in aid among the 12 Soviet successor states. A large part of this U.S. aid has supported Comprehensive Threat Reduction (CTR) programs to prevent the proliferation of weapons of mass destruction. Budgeted aid for FY2011 was $17.6 million and was $19.3 million for FY2012. Requested aid for FY2014 is $12.2 million (these latter amounts include foreign assistance listed in the *Congressional Budget Justification for Foreign Operations*, and exclude Defense and Energy Department funds; country totals have not been released for FY2013). The Administration states that Kazakhstan's significant progress "as a stable, secure, democratic, and prosperous partner [has] allowed the U.S. government to scale down funding levels in FY2014." The request for FY2014 emphasizes security programs ($4.8 million) such as Foreign Military Financing (FMF), International Military Education and Training (IMET), Non-Proliferation, Antiterrorism, Demining, and Related Programs (NADR), and International Narcotics Control and Law Enforcement (INCLE); economic support ($4.1 million) for developing small businesses, attracting more foreign investment, and increasing energy efficiency (these programs will be funded mostly by Kazakhstan with some U.S. support); and democracy support ($2.8 million) to strengthen judicial independence and bolster human rights and civil society NGOs.[68]

U.S. defense cooperation has included FMF, IMET, and other assistance and participation in annual Steppe Eagle military exercises in Kazakhstan (held under the aegis of NATO's Partnership for Peace). In July 2012, U.S. Secretary of the Navy Ray Mabus visited Kazakhstan and met with Defense Minister Dzhaksybekev. The two reportedly discussed the accomplishments of the 2008-2012 defense cooperation plan in the areas of training and equipment for the peacekeeping brigade, special forces training, technical assistance, and military education, and worked on drafting a new 2013-2017 plan. In April 2013, cadets from the U.S. Military Academy at West Point visited the Military Institute of Ground Forces, and during the SPC meeting in July 2013, the two sides discussed mutual visits by the defense minister/secretary.

Among congressional actions, Omnibus Appropriations for FY2003 (P.L. 108-7) forbade assistance to the government of Kazakhstan unless the Secretary of State determined and reported that Kazakhstan had significantly improved its human rights record during the preceding six-month period. The Secretary could, however, waive this prohibition on national security grounds. This language has been continued in yearly appropriations acts. Since FY2005, the Secretary of State (or the designee) has reported to Congress that Kazakhstan has failed to significantly improve its human rights record, but that aid restrictions have been waived on national security grounds.

Counter-Terrorism Support

With regard to Iraq, Kazakhstan's then-Foreign Minister Kasymzhomart Tokayev on March 28, 2003, voiced general support for disarming Iraq. Tokayev later explained that Kazakhstan had decided to support the coalition because it feared that Saddam Hussein was building weapons of mass destruction. Reportedly responding to a U.S. appeal, the Kazakh legislature in

May 2003 approved sending military engineers to Iraq. The 27 troops trained Iraqis in de-mining and water purification. Kazakh troops withdrew from Iraq in late 2008.

With regard to Afghanistan, President Nazarbayev warned in June 2001 that Taliban actions in Afghanistan increasingly threatened regional security, and after September 11 he offered overflight rights and the use of airbases to the U.S.-led coalition, but did not offer troops. Kazakhstan also facilitated the transshipment of supplies to U.S. bases in Uzbekistan and Kyrgyzstan. A U.S.-Kazakh memorandum of understanding was signed in July 2002 that permitted U.S. military aircraft to use Kazakhstan's Almaty airport for emergency military landings. In September 2003, a five-year military cooperation agreement was signed to combat terrorism, develop peacekeeping forces, bolster air defense capabilities, and enhance security in the Caspian Sea. In February 2008, the accord was extended to 2012. After receiving Kazakhstan's permission, in early 2009 NATO countries began rail shipments of nonlethal supplies to support the operations of the International Security Assistance Force (ISAF) in Afghanistan. A U.S.-Kazakh accord on over-flight rights for military equipment and personnel was brokered in April 2010. According to one source, U.S. military purchases of local goods and transit fees paid to regional states amount to several hundred million dollars annually.[69]

In October 2010, Kazakhstan and NATO reached agreement on detailing four Kazakh officers to ISAF headquarters, and the Majlis in May 2011 approved the agreement. Just before the Majilis approved the deployment, a suicide bombing took place in the city of Aktobe outside a security forces building, reportedly injuring two security personnel, and after the approval a car bomb detonated in Astana, similarly outside a security forces building, killing two people in the car. No one took immediate responsibility for the bombings, and it was unclear if they were linked to the Majilis action. Perhaps telling, just after the approval, the Taliban allegedly warned that the deployment would be regarded as "disloyal" and damaging to Kazakh-Taliban relations.[70] The Kazakh Senate (upper legislative chamber) then added qualifying language to the bill approved by the lower chamber and returned it to the Majlis, apparently reflecting a policy change by the government. The Senate explained its action as a response to widespread public opposition to sending military personnel to Afghanistan. Finally, in April 2013, the Kazakh Foreign Ministry announced that in light of ISAF's withdrawal from Afghanistan, the agreement had become irrelevant.

In early June 2012, NATO Secretary-General Anders Fogh Rasmussen announced that Kazakhstan, Kyrgyzstan, and Uzbekistan had agreed to allow the reverse transit of cargoes out of Afghanistan. At the "Istanbul Process" conference held in Kabul in mid-June to discuss support for post-2014 Afghanistan, Kazakhstan pledged to assist in disaster management, counter-narcotics, business, and educational confidence building measures, including to increase the number of Afghan students receiving university and vocational education in Kazakhstan.

Kazakhstan reportedly is advocating that the use of its Caspian seaport at Aktau be increased as a component of the NDN. Reportedly, the port already is used to transport thousands of containers to and from Afghanistan.

End Notes

[1] U.S. Embassy, Astana, Kazakhstan. Interview by ... Richard A. Boucher with Aybek Aldabergenov of Era TV, June 6, 2007.

[2] OSCE, Office for Democratic Institutions and Human Rights, Republic of Kazakhstan Parliamentary Elections, 18 August 2007: Election Observation Mission Report, October 30, 2007.

[3] Joanna Lillis, "Bill to Boost Nazarbayev's Powers in Kazakhstan Remains Theoretically Alive," Eurasianet, June 9, 2010.

[4] OSCE, Office for Democratic Institutions and Human Rights, International Election Observation, Republic Of Kazakhstan, Early Presidential Election, 3 April 2011: Statement of Preliminary Findings and Conclusions, April 4, 2011.

[5] U.S. Embassy, Astana, Kazakhstan, Press Release: U.S. Embassy Statement, April 4, 2011.

[6] CEDR, December 19, 2011, Doc. No. CEP-950019.

[7] OSCE, ODIHR, Republic Of Kazakhstan, Early Parliamentary Elections, 15 January 2012: OSCE/ODIHR Election Observation Mission Final Report, April 3, 2012.

[8] European Parliament, Resolution of 15 March 2012 on Kazakhstan, 2012/2553(RSP), March 15, 2012.

[9] U.S. Department of State, On-the-Record Briefing With International Media: Robert O. Blake, Jr., Assistant Secretary, Bureau of South and Central Asian Affairs, August 15, 2012.

[10] About the Abuses of Kazakhstan's Dictatorship and Its Ruler Nursultan Nazarbayev, Human Rights Foundation, October 17, 2012; Washington Examiner, October 17, 2012; Consulate General of the Republic of Kazakhstan in New York, Kazakhstan's Response to the Recent Ad in Washington Examiner, October 24, 2012; Joanna Lillis, "Kazakhstan: Nazarbayev Friends and Foes Sling Mud," Eurasianet, November 14, 2012.

[11] U.S. Department of State, Ambassador Kelly on Sentencing of Vladimir Kozlov in Kazakhstan, 11 October 2012.

[12] Joanna Lillis, "Kazakhstan: Political Trial Fails to Provoke Outcry," Eurasianet, October 10, 2012.

[13] "Main Opposition Media Silenced in Space of a Month," Reporters Without Borders, December 28, 2012, and January 2, 2013, at http://en.rsf.org/kazakhstan-main-opposition-media-silenced-in-28-12-2012,43751.html.

[14] "New 'Leader's Day' Suggests Power Consolidation Ahead of Handover," Open Source Center Analysis, November 30, 2012; Interfax, November 29, 2012.

[15] CEDR, November 9, 2011, Doc. No. CEP-950038; Interfax, November 30, 2011.

[16] Embassy of the Republic of Kazakhstan, Washington, DC, "Response to the Human Rights Watch Report," News Bulletin, September 18, 2012. The response is to Human Rights Watch, Striking Oil, Striking Workers: Violations of Labor Rights in Kazakhstan's Oil Sector, September 4, 2012. The News Bulletin claims that HRW ignored "facts" put forward by the Kazakh government, but HRW states that the Kazakh government did not respond to its request for information and alleges that the government attempted to block its investigation.

[17] CEDR, July 13, 2012, Doc. No. CEP-950108.

[18] CEDR, June 27, 2012, Doc. No. CEP-950051.

[19] CEDR, November 23, 2012, Doc. No. CEP-950005.

[20] Joanna Lillis, "Kazakhstan: Astana Mulls Expansion of Anti-Terror Controls," Eurasianet, June 19, 2013.

[21] U.S. House of Representatives, Committee on Foreign Affairs, Subcommittee on Europe, Eurasia, and Emerging Threats and Subcommittee on Terrorism, Nonproliferation, and Trade, Hearing on Islamic Militant Threats in Eurasia, Testimony of Robert Blake, February 27, 2013.

[22] World Report 2013, Human Rights Watch, January 31, 2013.

[23] U.S. Department of State. Country Reports on Human Rights Practices for 2012, April 19, 2013.

[24] U.S. Department of State, International Religious Freedom Report for 2012, May 20, 2013; Trafficking in Persons Report, June 19, 2013. In July 2013, President Nazarbayev signed into law amendments aimed at increasing criminal penalties against those involved in human trafficking. According to one report, the Kazakh Interior Ministry, among others, had urged broader penalties in the face of increasing numbers of cases of human trafficking. CEDR, June 25, 2013, Doc. No. CEN-38822765.

[25] Interfax, March 13, 2013.

[26] U.S. Department of State, United States Mission to the OSCE, Religious Freedom in Kazakhstan: As delivered by Ambassador Ian Kelly to the Permanent Council, April 11, 2013; CEDR, April 17, 2013, Doc. No. CEL-34140224.

[27] CEDR, April 17, 2013, Doc. No. CEL-34140224.

[28] The Moscow Times, July 1, 2013; Interfax, July 1, 2013.

[29] Old Habits: The Routine Use of Torture and Other Ill-Treatment in Kazakhstan, Amnesty International, July 11, 2013.

[30] OSCE, 15th Ministerial Council Meeting, Address of Marat Tazhin, Minister of Foreign Affairs of the Republic of Kazakhstan, November 29, 2007.

[31] An Atmosphere of Quiet Repression: Freedom of Religion, Assembly and Expression in Kazakhstan, Human Rights Watch, December 2008.

[32] Human Rights in Kazakhstan: Seven Months before the OSCE Chairmanship, Human Rights Watch Memorandum, Human Rights Watch, May 20, 2009.

[33] Commission for Security and Cooperation in Europe, Articles, OSCE 2010 Informal Ministerial: Kazakhstan Persistence Earns A Summit In Astana, by Winsome Packer, November 1, 2010.

[34] OSCE Permanent Council, Countdown to the OSCE Summit: Statement by Mr. Kanat Saudabayev, Chairperson-inOffice of the OSCE and Secretary of State and Minister for Foreign Affairs, November 15, 2010.

[35] United States Mission to the OSCE, Opening Plenary Session at the OSCE Review Conference, Vienna, Austria, As delivered by Dr. Michael Haltzel, U.S. Head of

Delegation, OSCE Review Conference, October 18, 2010; Closing Plenary Session of OSCE Review Conference in Vienna, Austria, As delivered by Dr. Michael Haltzel, October 26, 2010.

[36] United States Mission to the OSCE, OSCE Review Conference, Vienna, Austria, As delivered by Julie Raschka, October 25, 2010; Catherine Fitzpatrick, "Turkmen Activists Denied Entry to OSCE Review Conference in Warsaw," Eurasianet, October 4, 2010.

[37] CEDR, December 15, 2012, Doc. No. CEP-950064.

[38] Kazakhstan: Country Report, Economic Intelligence Unit, May 2011.

[39] U.S. Department of Commerce, Census Bureau, International Trade Statistics, at http://www.census.gov/foreigntrade/statistics/country/.

[40] Richard Weitz, "Kazakhstan Investment, Part 1: Europeans Dominate Inward Foreign Direct Investment," Eurasia Daily Monitor, January 18, 2013.

[41] Republic of Kazakhstan: 2013 Article IV Consultation Concluding Statement of the IMF Mission, International Monetary Fund, June 4, 2013.

[42] Doing Business 2013, World Bank, October 22, 2012; James Roberts and Ariel Cohen, How More Economic Freedom Will Attract Investment to Kazakhstan and Central Asia – Analysis, The Heritage Foundation, June 27, 2012.

[43] BP Statistical Review of World Energy, British Petroleum, June 2013.

[44] Kazakh Oil and Gas Ministry Hopes for Speedy Settling of Budget of Kashagan Field's First Phase," Trend News Agency, April 26, 2012; Robert Cutler, "Kashagan Costs Surge," Asia Times, January 21, 2012; Nariman Gizitdinov, "Biggest Find in Decades Becomes $39 Billion Cautionary Tale," Bloomberg, November 16, 2011.

[45] U.S. Department of State, Bureau of Economic and Business Affairs, 2013 Investment Climate Statement, February 2013. According to the report, "despite growing investment in Kazakhstan's energy sector, concerns remain about the government's tendency to challenge contractual rights, to legislate preferences for domestic companies, and to create mechanisms for government intervention in foreign companies' operations, particularly in procurement decisions. Together with vague and contradictory legal provisions that are often arbitrarily enforced, these negative tendencies feed a perception that Kazakhstan is a suboptimal investment environment."

[46] Press Release: Agreement Reached with Republic of Kazakhstan on Karachaganak, BG Group, December 14, 2011, at http://www.bg-group.com/MEDIACENTRE/PRESS/Pages/ 14Dec 2010.aspx.

[47] ITAR-TASS, May 29, 2008; CEDR, December 11, 2007, Doc. No. CEP-950096; April 26, 2008, Doc. No. CEP-950045.

[48] "Natural Gas: Trade Movements 2010," BP Statistical Review of World Energy, June 2011, p. 29.

[49] CEDR, October 22, 2009, Doc. No. CEP-950337.

[50] Interfax, October 6, 2011.

[51] CEDR, April 5, 2011, Doc. No. CEP-950102.

[52] CEDR, December 15, 2013, Doc. No. CEP-950064.

[53] CEDR, January 9, 2013, Doc. No. CEP-950123; March 7, 2013, Doc. No. CEL-17758744.

[54] The Military Balance, International Institute of Strategic Studies, March 14, 2013.

[55] Roger McDermott, "Kazakhstan's 2011 Military Doctrine and Regional Security Beyond 2014," CACI Analyst, June 13, 2012. However, a retired Kazakh military officer argued in an article in 2010 against doing away with the draft and moving to a volunteer force. K.S. Serikbayev, "The Armed Forces of the Republic of Kazakhstan: Problems and Possible Areas of Reform," Military Thought, July 1-September 30, 2010.

[56] CEDR, September 23, 2010, Doc. No. CEP-677004; June 4, 2010, Doc. No. CEP-37008; May 4, 2012, Doc. No. CEP-358004.

[57] The Military Balance, International Institute of Strategic Studies, March 14, 2013.

[58] The White House, Office of the Press Secretary, Joint Statement on the meeting between President Obama and Kazakhstan President Nazarbayev April 11, 2010.

[59] The White House, Office of the Press Secretary, Remarks by President Obama and President Nursultan Nazarbayev of the Republic of Kazakhstan Before Bilateral Meeting, March 26, 2012; Joint Statement of the Presidents of the Republic of Kazakhstan, the Russian Federation, and the United States of America Regarding the Trilateral Cooperation at the Former Semipalatinsk Test Site, March 26, 2012.

[60] U.S. Department of State, Office of the Spokesman, Remarks: Secretary of State Condoleezza Rice At Eurasian National University, October 13, 2005.

[61] Sean Roberts, Issue Brief: Kazakhstan and the United States: Twenty Years of Ambiguous Partnership, Atlantic Council, January 2012; Jeffrey Mankoff, The United States and Central Asia after 2014, Center for Strategic and International Studies, January 2013.

[62] U.S. Department of State, Congressional Budget Justification for Foreign Operations, Annex: Regional Perspectives, FY2014, May 17, 2013.

[63] Kazakhstan Embassy, Washington, D.C., Joint Statement: The Ninth Meeting of the U.S.-Kazakhstan Energy Partnership, October 16, 2012; Richard Weitz, "New Kazakhstan-U.S. Energy Partnership Plan Adopted," Eurasia Daily Monitor, November 2, 2012.

[64] U.S. Department of State, Introductory Remarks at Business Forum: U.S.-Kazakhstan Strategic Partnership Dialogue, Robert O. Blake, Jr., Assistant Secretary, Bureau of South and Central Asian Affairs, April 10, 2012; Kazakhstan Embassy, Washington, D.C., Erlan Idrissov, Kazakhstan-U.S. Strategic Partnership Commission/Dialogue's Inaugural Meeting Opens a New Avenue for Bilateral Cooperation, April 23, 2012

[65] U.S. Department of State, Office of the Spokesperson, Joint Statement of Second Kazakhstan-United States Strategic Partnership Dialogue, July 10, 2013.

[66] U.S. Department of State, On-the-Record Briefing With International Media: Robert O. Blake, Jr., Assistant Secretary, Bureau of South and Central Asian Affairs, August 15, 2012.

[67] U.S. House of Representatives, Committee on Foreign Affairs, Subcommittee on Europe and Eurasia, Hearing; U.S. Engagement in Central Asia, Testimony by Robert Blake, Assistant Secretary, Bureau of Central and South Asian Affairs, July 24, 2012. See also U.S. Department of State, Opening Remarks at Nazarbayev University, Robert O. Blake, Jr. Assistant Secretary, Bureau of South and Central Asian Affairs, April 23, 2013.

[68] U.S. Department of State, Congressional Budget Justification for Foreign Operations, Annex: Regional Perspectives, FY2014, May 17, 2013.

[69] Deirdre Tynan, "Central Asia: Who's the Big Winner in the NDN Sweepstakes?" Eurasianet, February 7, 2012; U.S. Department of Commerce. U.S. Commercial Service. Kazakhstan: Northern Distribution Network, April 23, 2010. Section 801 of the National Defense Authorization Act for FY2010 (P.L. 111-84) provides temporary authority to limit competition to, or provide a preference for, products and services that are from countries along the Northern Distribution Network in support of operations in Afghanistan when it is determined that it is in the national security interest of the United States. Other goals include bolstering the economies of the Central Asian states and regional integration.

[70] Open Source Center, South Asia: Daily Report, May 21, 2011, Doc. No. SAP-950023.

In: Kazakhstan ISBN: 978-1-62948-356-6
Editors: R. M. Hoyt and M. B. Weston © 2013 Nova Science Publishers, Inc.

Chapter 2

KAZAKHSTAN 2012 HUMAN RIGHTS REPORT*

U.S. Department of State; Bureau of Democracy, Human Rights and Labor

EXECUTIVE SUMMARY

The Republic of Kazakhstan has a government system dominated by President Nursultan Nazarbayev and the ruling Nur Otan Party. The constitution concentrates power in the presidency. The president controls the legislature and the judiciary as well as regional and local governments. Changes or amendments to the constitution require presidential consent. The 2012 national elections for the Mazhilis (lower house of parliament) fell short of international standards, as did the 2011 presidential election in which President Nazarbayev received 95 percent of the vote. Some security forces reported to civilian authorities; intelligence services reported to an army general who was appointed as head of the Ministry of Internal Affairs.

The most significant human rights problems were severe limits on citizens' rights to change their government; restrictions on freedom of speech, press, assembly, religion, and association; and lack of an independent judiciary

---

* This document was released by the U.S. Department of State; Bureau of Democracy, Human Rights and Labor, April 2013.

and due process, especially in dealing with pervasive corruption and law enforcement and judicial abuse.

Other reported abuses included: arbitrary or unlawful killings; military hazing that led to deaths; detainee and prisoner torture and other abuse; harsh and sometimes life-threatening prison conditions; arbitrary arrest and detention; infringements on citizens' privacy rights; restrictions on freedom of religion; prohibitive political party registration requirements; restrictions on the activities of nongovernmental organizations (NGOs); violence and discrimination against women; abuse of children; sex and labor trafficking; discrimination against persons with disabilities and ethnic minorities; societal discrimination against gay, lesbian, bisexual, and transgender (LGBT) persons and persons with HIV/AIDS; and child labor.

The government took modest steps to prosecute officials who committed abuses, especially in high-profile corruption cases; however, corruption was widespread and impunity existed, particularly for people with connections to government or law enforcement officials.

Section 1. Respect for the Integrity of the Person, Including Freedom from:

a. Arbitrary or Unlawful Deprivation of Life

There were reports that the government or its agents committed arbitrary or unlawful killings.

In December 2011 a seven-month strike of oil-workers in Zhanaozen and the nearby village of Shetpe disintegrated into violence between protesters and law enforcement officials, leaving at least 17 people dead and more than 100 injured. Videos posted online depicted law enforcement officials shooting into the crowds, chasing after fleeing protesters, and beating them with batons.

The government's efforts to hold individuals accountable for the violence raised concerns about due process, selective prosecutions, and the use of the court system to silence opposition voices and deter criticism of the government. In May the court sentenced five mid-level policemen to between five and seven years in prison for using excessive force in response to the events in Zhanaozen. They also were to be banned from working in law enforcement for five years upon their release from prison. The court sentenced the former director of the Zhanaozen police detention center to five years in prison and ordered him to compensate the family of a detainee who died after police beat him while in custody. A court sentenced three oil company managers to between seven and eight years in prison on financial corruption charges, which the government viewed as having escalated the social unrest and prolonged the oil workers' strike. In September the Special Inter District Court of Aktobe sentenced former mayor of Zhanaozen Orak Sarbopeyev to 10 years in prison for abuse of power and corruption.

In June the Aktobe regional court convicted 13 oil workers of instigating the violence, sentencing them to between three and seven years in prison. The court either acquitted or issued suspended sentences to an additional 24 workers (see section 1.c.). In October a court sentenced unregistered Alga party leader Vladimir Kozlov to seven and one-half years in prison for inciting social discord, calling for the violent overthrow of the government, and forming a criminal group in connection with the violence; most observers found the evidence against him unconvincing (see sections 1.d., 1.e., and 3).

Military hazing led to deaths, suicides, and serious injuries. In April a military court found Major Duman Aytkozhim, the deputy head of the Aktobe Military Unit, guilty of abuse of power in connection with the suicide of 20-year-old Private Olzhas Baytasov.

The investigation determined that when Major Aytkozhim found Baytasov talking on his cell phone, the major humiliated and threatened Baytasov and broke his mobile phone. The military court sentenced Aytkozhim to five and one-half years in prison and ordered him to pay 500,000 tenge ($3,333) in reparations to Baytasov's family. There were several other reports of suicides in response to hazing.

While the government did not publish statistics on the number of deaths specifically linked to hazing of military recruits during the year, authorities reported the number of suicides in the army increased from two in 2011 to eight in 2012.

There were deaths reported in prisons due to abuse (see section 1.c.).

b. Disappearance

There were no reports of disappearances during the year.

c. Torture and Other Cruel, Inhuman, or Degrading Treatment or Punishment

The law prohibits torture; nevertheless, police and prison officials allegedly tortured and abused detainees, often in an effort to obtain or force confessions. For example, a representative from the Kazakhstan International Bureau for Human Rights reported seeing physical signs of torture, including scabbed skin, open wounds, bruises, and evidence of exposure to extreme cold on prisoners. The representative also asserted that authorities generally did not allow human rights observers to observe conditions in penal colonies. Members of the Public Monitoring Commission, a group comprised of NGO representatives, interviewed prisoners in a Kostanai penal colony. After the interview, authorities confiscated the group's notes and reportedly punished prisoners who had submitted complaints to the commission by beating them and placing them in punitive cells.

According to local NGOs, torture most often occurred in pretrial detention centers in order to obtain confessions.

Authorities charged two police officers from the Saragash District in South Kazakhstan with torture while trying to obtain confessions from three detainees accused of theft. The police officers allegedly placed plastic bags over the detainees' heads and subjected them to electric shocks.

The Public Committee on Human Rights, created in 2007 in the city of Kostanai by several local NGOs and representatives from the unregistered political party Alga, reported it received numerous complaints of torture from the pretrial detention facility in Aktau City. Several of the oil workers accused of organizing mass rioting during the 2011 violent clashes between strikers and police in Zhanaozen alleged that police tortured them after they were arrested. Civil society activist Galym Ageleuov monitored the trial of the 37 oil workers and reported that Parakhat Dyusenbaev testified that on April 17 he was beaten, humiliated sexually, and threatened with rape and arson.

Human rights activists asserted that the legal definition of torture was too vague to meet UN standards and that the penalties for the crime were too lenient. They also asserted that in many cases perpetrators were charged with "abuse of power" rather than torture. The Kazakhstani Commission on Human Rights, which advises the president on human rights issues, reported in 2011 that some law enforcement officers used torture and other illegal methods of investigation. The commission stated that there were no independent institutions to effectively investigate complaints of torture.

The human rights ombudsman reviewed prisoner and detainee complaints and concluded that law enforcement officers used abuse or torture to gain confessions. The ombudsman can either issue a recommendation directly to the relevant agency or release a public statement, but cannot legally force agencies to comply with its recommendations. The Coalition of NGOs against Torture (CNGOT) also received complaints of torture during the year. The Prosecutor's Office did not address these complaints.

In September the Taldykorgan City Court acquitted six policemen accused of torturing detainees and instead convicted them of abuse of power, sentencing them to one year in prison and fining them 500,000 tenge ($3,333) each.

In October authorities fired the chief of the Starogorodsky Police Department in Temirtau and arrested three policemen in response to accusations that they detained and tortured two local residents. According to the Ministry of Interior, the police officers admitted using torture. The trial was not completed by year's end.

According to the Ministry of Defense, there were 24 cases of military hazing reported during the year, but no military officers were convicted of hazing. The ministry continued unannounced inspections and required systematic reports from senior officers about hazing in their units.

Prison and Detention Center Conditions

Prison conditions were harsh and sometimes life threatening, and facilities did not meet international health standards. Health problems among prisoners went untreated in many cases or were exacerbated by poor prison conditions. Medical care was inadequate.

Physical Conditions

According to the latest government statistics, there were approximately 6,410 prisoners and detainees in pretrial facilities. Abuse occurred in police cells, pretrial detention facilities, and prisons. Observers cited severe overcrowding, poor treatment of inmates and detainees, and the lack of professional training programs for administrators. According to Penal Reform International (PRI), there were 4,817 prisoners infected with HIV. The chair of the Criminal Corrective Committee, Zhanat Keshubayev, stated that there were 1,677 prisoners infected with HIV. Aigul Katrenova, head of the Committee of the State Sanitary-Epidemiology Inspectorate of the Ministry of Health, reported there were 27 fewer cases of HIV-infected prisoners than in the previous year. However, she identified the following as persisting problems: insufficient access to medical care, lack of monitoring of antiretroviral treatment of HIV-infected prisoners, shortage of medical personnel, lack of infectious disease doctors, and shortages in medication. PRI stated that there was a widespread lack of heating and adequate ventilation within the prison system.

Prisoners had access to potable water.

The government reported 39 deaths in pretrial detention centers and police cells, compared with 45 in 2011. PRI reported 220 deaths in prisons as a result of illness and 59 due to other reasons, including suicide.

The government reported 14 suicides in pretrial detention facilities and police cells in 2011. At year's end the figures had not been released for 2012.

Incidents of inmates' self-mutilation as a protest against harsh prison conditions and abuse increased considerably, with 340 cases reported during the year.

Administration

Although alternatives existed for sentencing nonviolent offenders, officials and NGOs noted they remained underutilized. During the year the government instituted a transfer of responsibility for prisoners' health care to the Ministry of Health from the Ministry of Justice. NGOs reported it was too soon to judge the efficacy of this measure but complained of lack of transparency in the process.

According to observers, prisoners and detainees generally had reasonable access to visitors. Human rights activists reported complaints that prison administrators interfered with prisoners' religious observance. The CNGOT reported an increase in all categories of complaints from prisoners.

Monitoring

Civil society activists worked with the councils for public oversight of the Ministry of Justice and the Ministry of Internal Affairs (MIA), as well as the human rights ombudsman's Counter-Torture Working Group, to monitor the situation in prisons and detention facilities. Many observers criticized the councils for lacking independence and clearly defined authority or power.

The International Committee of the Red Cross did not monitor prison conditions in the country.

d. Arbitrary Arrest or Detention

The law prohibits arbitrary arrest and detention, but problems remained.

Role of the Police and Security Apparatus

The MIA supervises the national police force, which has primary responsibility for internal security, including investigation and prevention of crimes and administrative offenses, and maintenance of public order and security. The Agency for Combating Economic and Corruption Crimes (Financial Police) has administrative and criminal investigative powers. The Committee for National Security (KNB) plays a role in border security, internal security, antiterrorism efforts, and the investigation and interdiction of illegal or unregistered groups, such as extremist groups, military groups, political parties, religious groups, and trade unions. The KNB, Syrbar (a separate foreign intelligence service), and the Financial Police report directly to the president.

Many government ministers maintained personal blogs where citizens could register complaints. During the year the then prime minister Massimov received 147,544 complaints on his personal blog. Minister of Internal Affairs Kalmukhanbet Kassymov received 147,542 complaints on his personal blog.

The prosecutor general chaired a council for coordination of law enforcement operations. Staff included heads of other law enforcement agencies. Among its many duties, the council reviewed complaints against law enforcement.

The MIA cooperated with NGOs to provide human rights training programs for local police. The government cooperated with international organizations to provide a limited number of law enforcement training courses aimed at decreasing abuse by emphasizing investigative skill development.

Arrest Procedures and Treatment While in Detention

Although the judiciary has the authority to restrict arrests, independent observers reported that judges usually authorized prosecutors' warrant requests. The Ministry of Justice reported 12,692 persons under procedural arrest in during the year, compared to 13,143 in 2011. During the year the courts authorized 11,263 or 95 percent of prosecutors' requests for warrant arrests, compared with 11,882 or 95.7 percent of requests in 2011. Prosecutors continued to have the power to authorize investigative actions, such as search and seizure.

Persons detained, arrested, or accused of committing a crime have the right to the assistance of a defense lawyer from the moment of detention, arrest, or accusation. The law does not require police to inform detainees that they have the right to an attorney, and in practice police did not do so. Human rights observers alleged that law enforcement officials dissuaded detainees from seeing an attorney, gathered evidence through preliminary questioning before a detainee's attorney arrived, and, in some cases, used corrupt defense attorneys to gather evidence. The law states that the government must provide an attorney for an indigent suspect or defendant when the suspect is a minor, has physical or mental disabilities, or faces serious criminal charges. In practice public defenders often lacked the necessary experience and training to assist defendants. The law bars defendants from freely choosing their defense counsel if the cases against them involve state secrets; it allows only lawyers who have special clearance to work on such cases.

Arbitrary Arrest

Prosecutors reported continuing problems with arbitrary arrest and detention of citizens. According to the Prosecutor General's Office, authorities released 668 persons illegally confined to pretrial detention centers and an additional 587 persons from holding centers at various law enforcement agencies.

The government frequently arrested and detained opponents and critics, sometimes for minor infractions such as unsanctioned assembly, which incurred either fines or 10 days of administrative arrest. According to the law, detainees may remain in pretrial detention for up to two months. Depending on the complexity and severity of the alleged offense, the term may be extended for up to one year while the investigation takes place. The pretrial detention term cannot be longer than the potential sentence for the offense. Authorities detained opposition activist Vladimir Kozlov for almost nine months while he awaited trial on charges related to the December 2011 unrest in Zhanaozen.

Pretrial Detention

The law allows police to hold a detainee for 72 hours before bringing charges. Human rights observers criticized this period as too lengthy and said that authorities often used this phase of detention to torture, beat, and abuse inmates to extract confessions. A bail system exists but was not used widely, and many individuals remained in pretrial detention until their trial. The law grants prisoners prompt access to family members; however, authorities sometimes sent prisoners to facilities located far from their homes and relatives, which restricted access for those who could not afford to travel.

Amnesty

After the passage of an amnesty bill in December 2011, authorities released 2,628 prisoners, reduced the prison sentences of 859 inmates, and dismissed more than 8,000 criminal cases. Human rights activist Evgeniy Zhovtis was granted amnesty in February, after serving two and one-half years of a four-year jail term.

e. Denial of Fair Public Trial

The law does not provide for an independent judiciary. The executive branch sharply limited judicial independence. Prosecutors enjoyed a quasi-judicial role and had the authority to suspend court decisions.

Corruption was evident at every stage of the judicial process. Although judges were among the most highly-paid government employees, lawyers and human rights monitors alleged that judges, prosecutors, and other officials solicited bribes in exchange for favorable rulings in the majority of criminal cases. In June the Special Inter District Criminal Court of the Akmola Oblast found two former judges of the Supreme Court, Saylaubek Dzhakishev and Almaz Tashenova, guilty of accepting and giving bribes.

Military courts have jurisdiction over civilian criminal defendants allegedly connected to military personnel undergoing a criminal trial. Military courts use the same criminal code as civilian courts.

Trial Procedures

All defendants enjoy a presumption of innocence and are protected from self-incrimination. Trials are public except in instances that could compromise state secrets or when necessary to protect the private life or personal family concerns of a citizen. Nevertheless, there were several reported cases of journalists and observers denied access to open court hearings. Only defendants charged with capital crimes are entitled to trial by jury.

During the April 5 trial of oil workers involved in the protests in Zhanaozen, the judge denied the request of the lawyer of one of the defendants, Gulnara Zhauspayeva, to allow journalists in the courtroom. The journalists were allowed to observe the trial via video monitors in another room, but they were unable to see the defendants.

Courts conducted jury trials for aggravated murder cases. Observers noted that the juror selection process was inconsistent and that judges, who deliberated with the jurors, tended to dominate the process. The Supreme Court reported that there were 142 jury trials in the first half of the year, in which 188 defendants were convicted and 14 were acquitted.

Defendants in criminal cases have the right to counsel and to a government-provided attorney if they cannot afford counsel. Under the criminal procedure code a defendant must be represented by an attorney when the defendant is a minor, has mental or physical disabilities, does not speak the language of the court, or faces 10 or more years of imprisonment. Defense attorneys reportedly participated in only half of all criminal cases, in part because the government did not provide sufficient funds to pay them. The law also provides defendants the right to be present at their trials, to be heard in court, to confront witnesses against them, and to call witnesses for the defense. They have the right to appeal a decision to a higher court. According to observers, defense attorneys played a minor role in trials, which were dominated by prosecutors.

Domestic and international human rights organizations reported numerous problems in the judicial system, including lack of access to court proceedings; lack of access to government-held evidence; frequent procedural violations; poor explanations of rights to defendants; denial of defense counsel motions; and failure of judges to investigate allegations that authorities extracted confessions through torture or duress. Activists called for the use of juries for a wider range of trials.

Lack of due process was a problem, particularly in a handful of politically motivated trials involving protests by opposition activists and in cases in which improper political or financial influence was alleged. For example, NGOs indicated the indictment in the case against Vladimir Kozlov contained lengthy political opinions and charges based on assumptions rather than evidence.

In building a criminal case against a defendant, human rights and international legal observers noted investigative and prosecutorial practices overemphasized a defendant's confession of guilt as against other types of evidence. Courts generally ignored allegations by defendants that officials had obtained confessions by torture or duress.

Political Prisoners and Detainees

On October 8, the Mangystau Inter District Court sentenced Vladimir Kozlov, leader of the unregistered opposition political party Alga, to seven and one-half years in prison for "forming a criminal group, inciting social discord, and calling for the violent overthrow of the constitutional order." The charges were linked to Kozlov's support of the striking oil workers in Zhanaozen. While Kozlov and Alga did provide the strikers with moral and financial assistance, authorities did not present evidence linking them to violence or the overthrow of the government to the court. The charge of inciting social discord was based on a strained interpretation of the law that established the government as a social group "analogous to a race, tribe, religion, or class." Most NGOs and international observers characterized the charges as politically motivated. The court also ordered the confiscation of all of Kozlov's personal property, most of which was used as office space and equipment for the Alga party.

In February authorities granted amnesty to human rights activist Evgeniy Zhovtis, who was convicted of vehicular manslaughter in 2009, stemming from an accident in which Zhovtis struck and killed a pedestrian. Local and international human rights NGOs contended that Zhovtis's sentence was politically motivated to silence a vocal critic of the government.

Civil Judicial Procedures and Remedies

Economic and administrative court judges handle civil cases under a court structure that largely mirrors the criminal court structure. The law and constitution provide for the resolution of civil disputes in court. In practice observers viewed civil courts as corrupt and unreliable. Observers noted litigants experienced difficulty having judgments enforced, particularly if they did not agree to pay a percentage of the proceeds to the court administrator.

f. Arbitrary Interference with Privacy, Family, Home, or Correspondence

The constitution and law prohibit privacy violations; however, the government at times infringed on these rights.

The law provides prosecutors with extensive authority to limit citizens' constitutional rights. The KNB, the MIA, the Financial Police, and other agencies, with the concurrence of the Prosecutor General's Office, may infringe on the secrecy of private communications and financial records, as well as on the inviolability of the home. Courts may hear an appeal of a prosecutor's decision but cannot issue an immediate injunction to cease an infringement. In June 2009 parliament amended the criminal procedure code to expand the range of cases in which police could wiretap and record communications without a warrant by allowing wiretapping in cases of medium gravity, as well as in urgent and grave ones, which was previously the standard.

Government opponents, human rights defenders, and their family members continued to report that the government occasionally monitored their movements and telephone calls.

SECTION 2. RESPECT FOR CIVIL LIBERTIES, INCLUDING

a. Freedom of Speech and Press

The constitution and the law provide for freedom of speech and of the press; however, the government used a variety of means to control the media and limit freedom of expression, including laws, harassment, licensing regulations, Internet restrictions, and criminal and administrative charges. Judicial actions against journalists and media outlets, including civil and criminal libel suits filed by government officials, led to the suspension of media outlets and self-censorship.

Freedom of Speech

The government limited individuals' ability to criticize the country's leadership; regional leaders attempted to limit local media outlets' criticism of them. The law prohibits insulting the president, the president's family, and other senior officials.

Freedom of Press

According to official statistics, the government owned 16 percent of the country's 2,783 media outlets. Many privately owned newspapers and television stations received government subsidies. Companies allegedly controlled by members of the president's family or loyal associates owned the majority of those broadcast media outlets that the government did not control outright. Media observers believed that the government wholly or partly owned most of the seven nationwide television broadcasters. Regional governments owned several frequencies, and the Ministry of Culture and Information (MCI) distributed them to independent broadcasters via a tender system.

All media were required to register with the MCI, although Web sites were exempt from this requirement.

The law limits the live retransmission of foreign-produced programming to 20 percent of a station's weekly airtime. This provision burdened smaller, less developed regional television stations that lacked resources to develop programs, although the government did not sanction any media outlet under this provision.

In November the Almaty Prosecutor's Office initiated cases demanding that several opposition media outlets be banned for allegedly "inciting social discord" and "calling for the overthrow of the constitutional order." The accused media outlets include the newspapers *Golos Respubliki*, *Vzglyad*, the Respublika Web portal, and the Internet television stations K Plus and Stan TV. At year's end various Almaty courts ruled in favor of the prosecutor's request to ban *Respublika, Golos Respubliki*, *Vzglyad*, K Plus, and Stan TV as extremist. In December the Almaty City prosecutor petitioned the court to suspend the Guljan.org opposition Web site for three months for allegedly calling for an unsanctioned demonstration. The court ordered Guljan.org to cease all operations until the case could be heard. At year's end the case continued.

Violence and Harassment

Press advocacy NGO Adil Soz recorded 15 attacks on editorial offices and journalists, compared with 14 in 2011. According to the NGO, reporters were prevented from carrying out their professional duties in 34 instances, compared with 43 the previous year, and journalists were denied or given significantly restricted access to public information 190 times. Journalists working in opposition media and those covering corruption reported harassment and intimidation by government officials and private actors.

On April 19, unknown assailants attacked Lukpan Akhmedyarov, a journalist from the newspaper *Uralskaya Nedelya*. The assailants beat him, stabbed him eight times, and shot him with an air gun. Akhmedyarov regained consciousness three days later. He believed that the attack was connected with his journalistic activity, and prompted by the publication of his article "Brother, Father of the Son-in-law and Pull," published a few weeks before the attack. The article detailed the personal relationships between members of government bodies in the Oblast of West Kazakhstan. The head of the Department of Internal Police Tlekkabyl Imashev sued Akhmedyarov and the newspaper for defamation. In July Akhmedyarov and the founder of *Uralskaya Nedelya* were charged with a fine of five million tenge ($33,333).

Censorship or Content Restrictions

The law enables the government to restrict media content under amendments that prohibit undermining state security or advocating class, social, race, national, or religious superiority, or cruelty and violence. Owners, editors, distributors, and journalists may be held civilly and criminally responsible for content unless it came from an official source. The government used this provision to limit media freedom.

The Uralsk City Court No. 2 ordered the newspaper *Uralskaya Nedelya* to pay 1.5 million tenge ($10,000) in damages to Arman Kozhakhmetov, who was the subject of one of the paper's articles. The article, written by journalist Lukpan Akhmedyarov and entitled "The Repeated Story," reported accusations from an alleged witness that several local city and law enforcement officials, including Kozhakhmetov, had participated in the murder of a famous athlete in 1999. The court ordered *Uralskaya Nedelya* and Akhmedyarov to publish an apology and retract the allegations. The case was under appeal at year's end.

Libel Laws/National Security

The law on state secrets makes it a criminal offense to release information regarding the health, finances, or private life of the president, as well as economic information, such as mineral reserves and government debts to foreign creditors. To avoid possible legal problems, media outlets often practiced self-censorship regarding the president or his family.

Private parties could initiate criminal libel suits without independent action by the government, and an individual filing such a suit is able to file a civil suit as well based upon the same allegations. Officials used the law's libel and defamation provisions to restrict media outlets from publishing unflattering information. Both the criminal and civil codes contain articles establishing broad liability for libel, with no statute of limitation or maximum amount of compensation. The requirement that owners, editors, distributors, publishing houses, and journalists prove the veracity of published information, regardless of its source, promoted self-censorship at each level.

In December 2011 Medeu District court in Almaty ordered the editor of the Web site Guljan.org, Gulzhan Yergaliyeva, to publish a retraction of statements made about the wife of the former chairman of the financial police, Saltana Akhanova. It also ordered Yergaliyeva to pay a fine of five million tenge ($33,333) as compensation for moral damages to Akhanova. Akhanova, wife of the former chairman of the financial police and current akim of the Akmolinsk Region Kayrat Kozhamzharov, filed a lawsuit against Yergaliyeva in response to an article published on Guljan.org that alleged Akhanova had millions of dollars in foreign bank accounts.

NGOs and monitors reported that libel cases against journalists and media outlets remained a problem. Adil Soz cited 16 criminal and 86 civil charges against media outlets and journalists during the first 10 months of the year, compared with 27 total suits in all of 2011.

The Law on National Security prohibits "the influence of information on public and individual consciousness related to deliberate distortion and spreading of unreliable information to the detriment of national security." According to experts, the term "unreliable information" is overly broad. The law also requires owners of communication networks and service providers to obey the orders of authorities in case of terrorist attacks or the government's order to enact the suppression of mass riots.

Publishing Restrictions

The law prohibits publication of any statement that promotes or glorifies "extremism," or "incites social discord," terms that international legal experts said the government had not clearly defined. The government subjected media outlets willing to criticize the president directly to intimidation, such as law enforcement actions or civil suits. Although these actions had a chilling effect on media outlets, criticism of government policies continued. Incidents of local government pressure on the media continued.

In September the MCI reported it had taken preventive steps to ensure no unofficial reports on emergencies leaked into the media. According to Minister of Culture Darkhan Mynbai, the ministry reached an agreement with state-owned media to ban any unofficial reports or negative interpretation of the official information during the time of an emergency. He also stated that the ministry would prevent the dissemination of any information from alternative sources during emergencies.

Internet Freedom

Observers reported that the government monitored e-mail and Internet activity, blocked or slowed access to opposition Web sites, and planted progovernment propaganda in Internet chat rooms. The state regulated the country's three internet service providers, including the state-owned Kaztelecom. Nevertheless, Web sites expressed a wide variety of views, including viewpoints critical of the government. The UN Broadband Communications Commission reported that 45 percent of the population had Internet access.

The MCI controlled the registration of ".kz" Internet domains. Authorities may suspend or revoke registration for failure to situate servers in the country. Observers criticized the registration process as unduly restrictive and vulnerable to abuse.

Adil Soz reported cases of the government blocking or restricting access to Web sites and the government's intermittent blocking of the Web site *LiveJournal* throughout the year, although the site remained accessible through other servers. Bloggers reported anecdotally that their sites were periodically blocked; including the independent news sites *guljan.org*, *respublika-kaz.info*, *kplustv.net*, *krasnoetv.kz*, *podkazt.kz*, *socialismkz.info*, and *janaozen.net*. Throughout the year the Committee to Protect Journalists reported that the Web site of the opposition newspaper *Golos Respubliki* remained inaccessible by users of Kaztelecom, the government-owned Internet service provider.

In December courts in Almaty banned several opposition news Web sites as extremist, including the official Web sites of the opposition newspapers *Vzglyad* and *Golos Respubliki*, as well as their social networking pages.

Courts frequently suspended the activities of opposition Web sites while the courts considered claims against them.

The government implemented new regulations on Internet access that mandated surveillance cameras in all Internet cafes, required visitors to present identification to use the Internet, demanded that Internet cafes keep a log of visited Web sites, and authorized law enforcement to access the names and Internet histories of users.

Academic Freedom and Cultural Events

The government generally did not restrict academic freedom, although academics, like other citizens, were prohibited from infringing on the dignity and honor of the president and his family. Many academics practiced self-censorship.

b. Freedom of Peaceful Assembly and Association

Freedom of Assembly

The law provides for limited freedom of assembly. There were significant restrictions on this right in practice, and police used force to disrupt peaceful demonstrations. For example, on May 1, Almaty police disrupted an unsanctioned Socialist Movement rally and struck activist Aynur Kurmanov in the head, forcing him to spend a week in the hospital. Authorities briefly detained and fined a number of activists. According to Kurmanov, authorities rejected all of the organization's more than 100 requests to protest during the year.

The law defines national security threats to include unsanctioned gatherings, public meetings, marches, demonstrations, illegal picketing, and strikes that upset social and political stability.

Under the laws governing public assembly, organizations must apply to local authorities for a permit to hold a demonstration or public meeting at least 10 days in advance. Opposition figures and human rights monitors complained that complicated and vague procedures and the 10-day notification period made it difficult for groups to organize public meetings and demonstrations, and they noted that local authorities turned down many applications for demonstrations or allowed them to take place only outside the city center.

Authorities often briefly detained and fined organizers of unsanctioned gatherings, including political party gatherings. For example, representatives from the unregistered opposition party Alga reported that authorities interfered with protests to boycott the April 2011 presidential election. The Kazakhstan International Bureau for Human Rights and Rule of Law, which monitors demonstrations in the seven largest cities, recorded 162 peaceful demonstrations from July 2011 to April 2012, 92.5 percent of which were unsanctioned. During that period the government sanctioned 12 demonstrations, including by progovernment groups. When the government did sanction public protests, it frequently designated locations in less populous areas outside the city center. In 12 cases authorities

physically prevented protesters from meeting. In nine cases authorities detained participants of unsanctioned demonstrations and later charged them with administrative violations. Overall, however, the organization noted an increase in the civic activities of citizens and a decrease in the number of cases where police prevented peaceful demonstrations.

The National Human Rights Action Plan for 2009-12 noted that the country's legal norms on public gatherings at times contradicted international standards, but the government has not introduced changes recommended in the plan.

Freedom of Association

The law provides for limited freedom of association. There were significant restrictions on this right in practice. Any public organization set up by citizens, including religious groups, must be registered with the Ministry of Justice, as well as with ministry branches in every region in which the organization conducts activities. The law requires public or religious associations to define their specific activities, and an association that acts outside the scope of its charter may be warned, fined, suspended, or ultimately prohibited. Participation in unregistered public organizations may result in administrative or criminal liability, such as fines, dissolution, probation, or imprisonment.

The prohibition on unregistered organizations often provided a pretext for authorities to interfere with the activities of organizations. "Membership organizations" other than religious groups, which are covered under separate legislation, must have 10 members in order to register at the local level and must have branches in more than half the country's regions for national registration. The government considered political parties and labor unions to be membership organizations but had additional specific registration requirements for them. The law requires 40,000 signatures for registration. If authorities challenge an application by alleging irregular signatures, the registration process can continue so long as the total number of eligible signatures remains above the minimum. The law prohibits parties established on an ethnic, gender, or religious basis. The law prohibits members of the armed forces, employees of national security and law enforcement organizations, and judges from participating in trade unions or political parties.

NGOs reported that the NGO registration process was straightforward, although corruption in the process was common. NGOs involved in human rights advocacy and political activities faced greater administrative delays and obstacles, although there were no reports that the government denied registration or closed organizations.

c. Freedom of Religion

See the Department of state's *International Religious Freedom Report* at www.state.gov/j/drl/irf/rpt.

d. Freedom of Movement, Internally Displaced Persons, Protection of Refugees, and Stateless Persons

The law provides for freedom of movement within the country, foreign travel, emigration, and repatriation, and despite some regulatory restrictions, the government generally respected these rights in practice. The government cooperated with the Office of the UN High Commissioner for Refugees (UNHCR) and other humanitarian organizations to provide protection and assistance to internally displaced persons, refugees, returning refugees, asylum seekers, stateless persons, and other persons of concern.

In-country Movement

The government required citizens and foreigners who remained in the country for more than five days to register with migration police. Foreigners who entered the country had to register at certain border posts. Registration in most of the country generally was routine; nonetheless, some foreign citizens reported that local authorities occasionally requested bribes before completing registration. Migration police routinely checked the registration of foreigners, including labor migrants, and reportedly requested bribes. Some foreigners experienced problems travelling to regions outside their registration area. In 2011 amendments to the law on migration eased registration requirements for ethnic Kazakh returnees (oralmans). A 2011 agreement on the legal status of migrant workers granted an exemption for families of migrant workers from registration for a 30-day period after the worker started employment. The new migration law granted the government the authority to deport those who violate the regulations, while the previous law restricted deportation to certain cases.

The government did not report on the number of foreigners deported for gross violation of visitor rules during the year. During the first nine months of 2011, the Ministry of Internal Affairs deported 12,644 foreigners for alleged gross violations of the visitor rules, the majority of whom were citizens of countries in the Commonwealth of Independent States (CIS). Individuals facing deportation can request asylum if they fear persecution in their home country. The government required persons who were suspects in criminal investigations to sign statements that they would not leave their place of residence and detained individuals routinely for identity checks without suspicion of a criminal offense.

Foreign Travel

Although the government did not require exit visas for the temporary travel of citizens, there were certain instances in which the government could deny exit from the country, including for travelers subject to pending criminal or civil legal proceedings, unfulfilled prison sentences, or compulsory military duty. Travelers who presented false documentation during the exit process could be denied exit, and authorities controlled travel by active-duty military personnel. The law on national security requires that persons who had access to state secrets obtain permission from their employing government agency for temporary exit from the country.

Emigration and Repatriation

The law provides for the right to emigrate and the right to repatriate, and the government generally respected these rights in practice. An exception is the law on national security, which prohibits persons who had access to state secrets from taking up permanent residence abroad for five years after leaving government service. The government required a permanent exit visa for emigration; obtaining this visa required criminal checks, credit checks, and letters from parents and any dependents over the age of 10 expressing no objection to exit visa issuance.

Authorities required foreigners to obtain prior permission to travel to certain border areas with China and cities in close proximity to military installations. The government continued to declare particular areas closed to foreigners due to their proximity to military bases and the space launch center at Baikonur. In practice foreigners could visit these areas with prior permission from the Ministry of Internal Affairs.

Protection of Refugees

The government cooperated with the UNHCR and other organizations to provide some protection and assistance to refugees from countries where their lives or freedom would be threatened on account of their race, religion, nationality, membership in a particular social group, or political opinion.

Access to Asylum

The country's laws provide for the granting of asylum or refugee status, and the government has established a system for providing protection to refugees. The law does not prohibit forced exile if authorized by an appropriate government agency or through a court ruling. The UNHCR legally can appeal to the government and interfere on behalf of an individual if facing deportation. The law on refugees, which a number of regulations and by-laws implement, regulates the granting of asylum and refugee status.

Access to Basic Services

The law on refugees outlines refugee status determination (RSD) procedures and access to state services, including the right to be registered and to be issued documents. The Committee on Migration under the Ministry of

Labor and Social Protection conducts RSDs. Observers stated that committee representatives suffered from lack of expertise, which the UNHCR attributed to rushed implementation of the law. The law stipulates that refugees have the right to education and social services, but administrative regulations and the prohibitive cost of the services to refugees often precluded the exercise of this right in practice. Authorities formed an interministerial working group with UNHCR to address these problems.

The government generally registered asylum seekers and determined their status in consultation with UNHCR. In some cases the government allowed asylum seekers and refugees to stay in the country while UNHCR found third countries that would accept them. Although the government performed refugee status determinations and registered refugees present in the country, it did not accept any refugees for resettlement from third countries, nor did it facilitate local integration (including naturalization) of refugees on its territory.

In September the government detained Uzbek refugee Makset Djabbarbergenov in response to an extradition request by the government of Uzbekistan, accusing him of conducting illegal religious activity. He remained in detention for approximately three months while the government considered his case. In December, after discussing the situation with many international actors including UNHCR and the International Organization for Migration (IOM), the government released Djabbarbergenov for resettlement in a third country.

Temporary Protection

The government also provided temporary protection to approximately five individuals during the year, including some Afghans, who might not qualify as refugees.

During the year the UNHCR reported generally cordial relations with the government in assisting refugees and asylum seekers. The government usually allowed the UNHCR access to detained foreigners to ensure proper treatment and fair determination of status. The government was generally tolerant in its treatment of local refugee populations, except for a few citizens from former Soviet republics. The government often did not allow refugees without passports or those who had entered the country illegally to register.

The Committee on Migration in the Ministry of Labor and Social Protection reviewed refugee claims, with the UNHCR and a local NGO, Kazakhstan International Bureau for Human Rights, participating as observers. Consistent with the Minsk Convention on Migration within the CIS, the government did not recognize Chechens as refugees. Chechens were eligible for temporary legal resident status for up to 180 days, as are any other CIS citizens. This temporary registration was renewable, but local migration officials have discretion over the renewal process. In some cases they solicited bribes, exploiting the vulnerability of Chechens due to their inability to return safely to Chechnya. The government has an agreement with China not to tolerate the presence of ethnic separatists from one country on the territory of the other. Human rights monitors remained concerned about the effect of this agreement on Uighurs from China living in the country, especially following the April 2010 transfer of RSDs for Uighurs from the UNHCR to the government. The government did not forcibly return any refugees protected under the UNHCR's mandate.

Stateless Persons

Estimates of the number of stateless people in Kazakhstan vary. According to official government statistics, between 7,000 and 8,000 officially recognized stateless persons resided in the country. The Ministry of Justice estimated that the actual number of stateless persons was approximately 21,000, while 57,000 persons self-identified as stateless in the 2009 census. Stateless people were generally holders of Soviet passports who failed to renew their documents after independence, ethnic Kazakh repatriates, and labor migrants. Although provided with the same rights as individuals with resident permits, stateless persons reported difficulty finding legal employment and had limited access to education and health care. The UNHCR continued to work with government and parliamentary officials to obtain reliable data on stateless persons and improve the country's citizenship legislation.

SECTION 3. RESPECT FOR POLITICAL RIGHTS: THE RIGHT OF CITIZENS TO CHANGE THEIR GOVERNMENT

The constitution and law provide for a democratic government with universal suffrage for those older than 18 years of age; in practice the government severely limited the right of citizens to change their government.

Although 2007 constitutional amendments increased legislative authority in some spheres, the constitution continues to concentrate power in the presidency. The president appoints and dismisses most high-level government officials, including the prime minister, the cabinet, the prosecutor general, the

KNB chief, Supreme Court and lower-level judges, regional governors, and the chairman and two members of the Central Election Commission (CEC), which oversees presidential and parliamentary elections. The lower house of parliament must confirm the president's choice of prime minister, and the senate must confirm the president's choice of prosecutor general, chief of the KNB, Supreme Court judges, and the head of the national bank. The parliament has never failed to confirm a presidential nomination. Modifying or amending the constitution effectively requires the president's consent. The 2007 constitutional amendments exempt President Nazarbayev from the two-term presidential term limit, and an amendment passed in 2010 gives him protection from prosecution. Two 2010 laws termed "Leader-of-the-Nation laws" establish President Nazarbayev as chair of the Kazakhstan People's Assembly, grant him lifetime membership on the Constitutional and Security Councils, allow him "to address the people of Kazakhstan at any time," and stipulate that all "initiatives on the country's development" must be coordinated through him.

Elections and Political Participation

Recent Elections

In November 2011 President Nazarbayev dismissed the lower house of parliament and called for early parliamentary elections on January 15. The early election resulted in the formation of a multiparty parliament, with the president's party, Nur Otan, holding the majority of the seats. No parties considered to oppose the president were elected. According to the Organization for Security and Cooperation in Europe (OSCE), the competitiveness and pluralism of the electoral environment was undermined because the government barred several political parties and candidates from competing. Many OSCE monitors reported instances of ballot stuffing, carousel voting, and proxy voting. The OSCE's assessment was that the election "did not meet fundamental principles of democratic elections."

Political Parties

Political parties must register members' personal information, including date and place of birth, address, and place of employment. This requirement discouraged many citizens from joining political parties. There were credible allegations that authorities pressured persons entering government service to join the Nur Otan party. At year's end there were 10 registered political parties, including the parties Ak Zhol, Rukhaniyat, and Auyl. These parties did not generally oppose President Nazarbayev's policies. In April the appellate court of Kokshetau City extended the six-month suspension of the Communist Party for an additional six months, reportedly on the grounds that a local press article naming the party's first secretary was proof the party had failed to honor its suspension. Additionally the effort of political parties Azat and the National Socialist Democratic Party (NSDP) to register as a joint party failed, with Azat losing its status as a registered political party. The unregistered political party Alga, which has sought registration since 2006, failed to achieve registration status. In November the Alga Party leader Vladimir Kozlov was sentenced to seven and one-half years in prison for creating and leading a criminal organization, inciting social discord , and calling for the violent overthrow of the government in connection to the support he and his party gave to striking oil workers prior to the 2011 violence in Zhanaozen. The Almaty prosecutor's office used the verdict against Kozlov to petition the court to ban Alga, the Khalyk Maidany political movement, and several opposition media outlets as extremist. The courts declared all of these organizations as extremist and banned their activities in the country's territory. Appeals of these rulings continued at year's end. In order to register, a political party must hold a founding congress with minimum attendance of 1,000 delegates from two-thirds of the oblasts and the cities of Astana and Almaty. Parties must obtain at least 700 signatures from each oblast and the cities of Astana and Almaty, registration from the CEC, and registration from each oblast-level election commission.

Participation of Women and Minorities

Traditional attitudes sometimes hindered women from holding high office or playing active roles in political life, although there were no legal restrictions on the participation of women or minorities in politics. At year's end there were two female ministers; 27 members of the Mazhilis (lower house of parliament) and two Senators were women.

SECTION 4. CORRUPTION AND LACK OF TRANSPARENCY IN GOVERNMENT

The law provides criminal penalties for official corruption; however, the government did not implement the law effectively, and officials frequently engaged in corrupt practices with impunity. Corruption was widespread in the executive branch, various law enforcement agencies, local government administrations, the education system, and the judiciary. The MIA, the Financial Police, the KNB, and the Disciplinary State Service Commission are responsible for combating corruption. Opposition leaders and human rights NGOs accused the government of rampant corruption.

Although authorities arrested two Supreme Court justices and the head of the customs agency on corruption charges, the government generally focused on lower to middle-ranking officials and minor political figures. The government did not release statistics on corruption during the year. In the first 11 months of 2011, courts convicted 24 government officials and 78 police officers of corruption. According to Supreme Court Chairman Bektas Beknazarov, 16 judges were fired for incompetence during the year. The government did not report the number of judges convicted of corruption.

According to the law on the "Fight Against Corruption," government officials, applicants for government positions, and those recently released from their jobs are required annually to declare their income and assets in Kazakhstan and abroad to tax authorities. The same requirement applies to their spouses, dependents, and adult children. Similar regulations exist for members of parliament and judges.

The law mandates that the government, public associations, officials, and media outlets provide citizens with information that affects their rights and interests; in practice citizens' requests for information were not fulfilled in a timely manner. NGOs reported problems with access to information from state agencies and cited red tape, poor content on official Web sites, and long lines in state agencies. According to an assessment by the local branch of Transparency International, all governmental ministries received poor transparency ratings except for the MCI, which was evaluated as average.

Although parliament published several draft laws, some parliamentary debates, and occasionally its voting record, many parliamentary activities took place outside public view. Accredited journalists and representatives of public associations could observe some parliamentary sessions via video link from a separate room. Transcripts of parliamentary sessions were not available to the public. During the year parliament barred the public and media from attending discussions of controversial legislation.

Section 5. Governmental Attitude Regarding International and Nongovernmental Investigation of Alleged Violations of Human Rights

A number of domestic and international human rights groups generally operated effectively, with relative freedom to investigate and publish their findings on human rights cases. However, some government restrictions on domestic and international human rights NGO activities remained. International and local human rights groups reported that the government continued to monitor the activities of NGOs that worked on sensitive issues and noted government harassment, including police visits and surveillance, of NGO offices, personnel, and family members.

Television channel KTK's program "Weekly Portrait" featured an episode that spoke out against several international NGOs, including Freedom House, National Democratic Institute, and Human Rights Watch. The program accused the organizations of supporting the violence in Zhanaozen. A separate program accused international NGOs, and specifically Freedom House, of supporting nontraditional religious sects.

The Almaty Helsinki Commission, the Republican Network of Independent Monitors, the Kazakhstani International Bureau for Human Rights, PRI, and Adil Soz were among the most active local human rights NGOs and occasionally faced difficulties in registering and acquiring office space and technical facilities. They also reported that the government audited their records and imposed various legal constraints to their activities. Multiple NGO activists reported heightened government monitoring prior to the first anniversary of the December 2011 violence in Zhanaozen. In some instances government agents misrepresented themselves to attend and monitor NGO events. The government continued to participate in--and include NGOs in--roundtables and events on democracy and human rights.

NGOs affiliated or suspected of being affiliated with the opposition reported harassment.

UN and Other International Bodies

In general the government did not prevent international NGOs and multilateral institutions dealing with human rights from visiting the country and meeting with local human rights groups and government officials. The government cooperated with the OSCE and its field mission. The UN, the IOM, and the Red Crescent Society also operated freely in the country.

National security laws prohibit foreigners, international organizations, NGOs, and other nonprofit organizations from engaging in political activities. The law stipulates that a noncommercial organization must provide information to tax authorities on its founders, activities, and foreign sources of funding, as well as income, property, expenses, and employee records. The law prohibits international organizations from funding unregistered entities.

Government Human Rights Bodies

The Presidential Commission on Human Rights is a consultative and advisory body that includes members of the public appointed by the president. The commission reviews and investigates complaints, issues recommendations, monitors fulfillment of international human rights conventions, and publishes annual human rights reports in close cooperation with several international organizations, such as the UNHCR, OSCE, IOM, and UNICEF. During the year the commission received approximately 2,000 written and oral complaints. The commission does not have legal authority to remedy human rights violations or implement its recommendations.

The presidentially appointed human rights ombudsman investigated approximately 1,300 complaints by citizens of violations of their rights by state agencies, although the ombudsman was not authorized to investigate complaints concerning the president, heads of government agencies, the parliament, the cabinet, the Constitutional Council, the Prosecutor General's Office, the CEC, or the courts. The ombudsman's office has the authority to appeal to the president, cabinet, or parliament to resolve citizens' complaints; cooperate with international human rights organizations and NGOs; meet with government officials concerning human rights violations; visit certain facilities, such as military units and prisons; and publicize the results of investigations in the media. The ombudsman's office also published an annual human rights report. During the year the office occasionally briefed the media and issued reports discussing complaints it had investigated.

Domestic human rights observers noted that although government human rights investigators advanced human rights in the country by publicizing statistics and individual cases, and aided citizens with less-controversial social problems and issues involving lower-level elements of the bureaucracy, the ombudsman's office and the human rights commission were unable to stop human rights abuses or punish perpetrators. The commission and the ombudsman avoided addressing underlying structural problems that led to human rights violations.

Section 6. Discrimination, Societal Abuses, and Trafficking in Persons

The law prohibits discrimination based on race, gender, disability, language, or social status; however, the government did not effectively enforce the law. Violence against women, trafficking in persons, and discrimination against nonethnic Kazakhs in government, persons with disabilities, and those in the LGBT community were problems.

Women

Rape and Domestic Violence

The law criminalizes rape. The punishment for rape, including spousal rape, ranges from three to 15 years' imprisonment. Out of 1,715 officially reported rape cases during the first nine months of the year, courts convicted 1,821 persons of criminal rape. Under the law, a prosecutor cannot initiate a rape case absent aggravating circumstances, such as gang rape, unless the victim files a complaint. Once a complaint is filed, the criminal investigation cannot be dismissed if the rape victim recants or refuses to cooperate further with the investigation. This provision was intended to protect victims from coercion. There were anecdotal reports of police and judicial reluctance to act on reports of rape, particularly in spousal rape cases.

Violence against women, including domestic violence, was a problem. Legislation identifies various types of domestic violence, such as physical, psychological, sexual, and economic, and outlines the responsibilities of the local and national governments and NGOs in providing support to domestic violence victims. The law also outlines mechanisms for issuance of restraining orders and provides for 24-hour administrative detention of abusers. The criminal procedure code sets the maximum sentence for spousal assault and battery at 10 years in prison, which is the same as for any assault.

NGOs maintain that the domestic violence law does not have an effective mechanism for implementation. According to NGOs, domestic violence remained a serious problem. Although official statistics were scarce, activists estimated that one in four families suffered domestic violence. During the year the government registered 80,571 crimes against women.

Police intervened in family disputes only when they believed the abuse was life threatening. According to NGO estimates, police investigated approximately 10 percent of cases of life-threatening abuse. NGOs conducted training for police officers on how to handle victims of domestic violence.

NGOs reported that women often withdrew their complaints because of economic insecurity. When victims pressed charges for domestic violence or spousal rape, police occasionally tried to persuade them not to pursue a case. When domestic violence cases came to trial, the charge was most often light battery, for which judges sentenced domestic abusers to incarceration at a minimum-security labor colony and 120 to 180 hours of work. Sentences for more serious cases of battery, including spousal battery, range from three months to three years of imprisonment; the maximum sentence for aggravated battery is 10 years' imprisonment.

Although the government stated that 29 crisis centers assist women and two centers assist men, NGOs reported that the number of active centers was much smaller. All the crisis centers received funding through government and international grants to NGOs. A number of smaller NGOs assisted victims, and six of the crisis centers provided shelter for victims of violence.

Sexual Harassment

Sexual harassment remained a problem. The law prohibits some forms of sexual harassment, but legal and gender experts regarded the legislation as inadequate. There were reports of incidents of harassment, but in no instance was the law used to protect the victim, nor were there reports of any cases prosecuted.

Reproductive Rights

Couples and individuals had the right to decide the number, spacing, and timing of their children and have the means to do so free from discrimination, coercion, or violence. Modern contraceptive methods were widely available. Women and men received equal treatment for sexually transmitted infections. Skilled personnel attended almost all births and provided at least one postnatal care visit, according to the Population Reference Bureau. According to the

Ministry of Health, the maternal mortality ratio was 13.3 deaths per 100,000 live births in 2011.

Discrimination

The constitution and law provide for equal rights and freedoms for men and women. The gender equality law defines the terms "gender," "gender equality," "sexual discrimination," and "equal opportunity" and prohibits discrimination based on gender. Despite the law, NGOs reported that no government body assumed responsibility for implementing the legislation and that the definition of gender discrimination did not comply with international standards. More women than men were self-employed or under-employed relative to their education level. According to observers, women in rural areas faced greater discrimination than women in urban areas and suffered from a greater incidence of domestic violence, limited education and employment opportunities, limited access to information, and discrimination in their land and property rights. According to the World Bank's Women, Business and the Law report, women in the country faced discrimination obtaining work in the same industries as men, and there were no laws protecting women from sexual harassment in the workplace.

Children

Birth Registration

Citizenship is derived both by birth within the country's territory and from one's parents. The government has a duty to register all births immediately.

Education

Education is mandatory through 16 years of age or secondary school; elementary schooling generally begins at age six. Primary and secondary education is free and universal. The law provides for access to public education for refugee and illegal migrant children. In some cases these children were denied access to schools, or their parents did not enroll them due to fear of discovery and deportation.

Child Abuse

There were reports of child abuse. NGOs estimated that more than half of all children younger than 14 experienced at least one incident of physical or psychological abuse by adults. Abuse was more common in rural areas.

According to the Ministry of Education, courts terminated the custody rights of approximately 782 abusive parents. According to the Ministry of Interior, in the first 10 months of the year 21 criminal cases were initiated against parents charged with criminal abuse. Minors who are 16 or older have the right to file petitions related to their interests directly with a court.

The president of the NGO Union of Crisis Centers stated that the number of psychological abuse cases exceeds the number of physical abuse cases. In the first 11 months of the year, the Union of Crisis Centers' hotline for children received 3,730 calls regarding child abuse, 60 percent of which were complaints about abused girls.

Child Marriage

The legal minimum age for marriage is 18 years. However, it may be reduced to 16 years in the case of pregnancy or with the consent of the parents or legal guardian. NGOs noted several cases of underage marriage, especially in the southern part of the country. Traditionally couples first married in mosques, and when the bride reached the legal age, the marriage would be registered officially.

Sexual Exploitation of Children

The minimum age for consensual sex is not specified in any article of the criminal code, but an article provides for eight to 15 years in prison as punishment for individuals who force boys or girls under the age of 18 to have sexual intercourse.

In 2010 the country introduced a criminal statute on the production and distribution of child pornography and expanded administrative penalties to cover the sale of pornographic materials to minors. The country retains administrative penalties for child pornography.

Displaced Children

According to the Ministry of Education, 3,984 children were identified as "street children" during the year. According to media reports, police placed homeless children in institutions run by the Ministry of Education for delinquent and street children. There they received medical and psychological assistance before they were released or sent to orphanages. During the year authorities sent 3,941 back to their families and placed 25 children in orphanages and institutions for children deprived of parental care.

Institutionalized Children

NGOs reported a high number of incidents of violence against children in orphanages, boarding schools, and detention facilities for delinquent children, and there were increased media reports of abuses in orphanages and other institutions. NGOs stated that half of children in orphanages or closed institutions suffered from abuse by teachers or other children.

International Child Abduction

The country is a not a party to the 1980 Hague Convention on the Civil Aspects of International Child Abduction.

Anti-Semitism

Approximately 30,000 to 40,000 Jews lived in the country. There were no reports of anti-Semitic acts apart from the distribution of anti-Semitic literature by Hizb ut-Tahrir. Leaders of the Jewish community reported no incidents of anti-Semitism by the government or in society.

Trafficking in Persons

See the Department of State's *Trafficking in Persons Report* at www.state

Persons with Disabilities

According to the Ministry of Labor and Social Protection, in 2011 there were 506,000 persons with disabilities (3 percent of the total population) in the country, although analysts argued that the real number was higher. The law prohibits discrimination against persons with physical, sensory, intellectual, and mental disabilities in employment, education, access to health care, and in the provision of other state services or other areas, but significant discrimination existed in the areas of employment, education, and access to government services.

The law provides for access to information for persons with disabilities. The government produced periodicals, scientific journals, reference literature, and fictional works that were recorded either on disk or in Braille. The law requires one national television channel to broadcast news programs with sign-language translation. NGOs stated that implementation of the laws on disability was lacking, and the Nur Otan party's Institute of Parliamentary Development concluded that access for disabled persons to information and communications was insufficient.

The law requires companies to set aside 3 percent of their jobs for persons with disabilities. International and local observers noted some improvement regarding the rights of persons with disabilities. Nevertheless, there were reports that persons with disabilities faced difficulty integrating into society and finding employment. According to Ministry of Labor and Social Protection, 3,400 persons with disabilities registered for employment, but only 1,762 were employed. The law mandates access to buildings for persons with disabilities. Vice Minister of Labor and Social Protection Assel Nusupova identified the two biggest problems facing persons with disabilities as poor infrastructure and lack of access to education. Persons with disabilities had difficulty accessing public transportation. The government did not make a concerted effort to address these problems.

Citizens with mental disabilities could be committed to state-run institutions without their consent or judicial review. In practice the government committed persons at a young age with the permission of their families. Institutions were poorly managed and inadequately funded.

There are no regulations regarding the rights of patients in mental hospitals. Human rights observers believed this led to mass abuse of patients' rights. NGOs reported that patients often were drugged and isolated for minor infractions and that they experienced poor conditions and a complete lack of privacy. In 2011 prosecutors disclosed violations of mental patients' rights ranging from illegal institutionalization to restricting access to information and unlawful extension of patients' stays. Prosecutors punished some officials as a result of the investigation. NGOs reported that orphanages for children with physical and mental disabilities were overcrowded and unsanitary, with insufficient staff to care adequately for children's needs.

The government did not restrict the right of persons with disabilities to vote and arranged home voting for individuals who could not travel to polling places as a result of their disability.

The Ministry of Labor and Social Protection was the primary government agency responsible for protecting the rights of persons with disabilities; the Ministries of Health and Education also assisted in their protection. Statistics on disability issues were unavailable.

National/Racial/Ethnic Minorities

The government continued to favor placing ethnic Kazakhs in senior government employment.

Ethnic Kazakh migrants who returned to the country from abroad experienced problems with housing, employment, and access to social services partly due to inadequate staffing and funding to meet their needs.

Kazakh is the official state language, although organizations and bodies of local self-administration officially may use Russian on an equal basis with Kazakh. By law the ability to speak Kazakh is not required for entry into the civil service, and there should be no discrimination on the basis of language, but Kazakh language ability was looked upon favorably. Non-Kazakh speakers protested that this was language discrimination. The Election Law requires presidential candidates to be fluent in Kazakh.

The creation of Kazakh language schools and the conversion of some Russian language schools to Kazakh reduced the overall number of Russian only-language schools.

Societal Abuses, Discrimination, and Acts of Violence Based on Sexual Orientation and Gender Identity

Although there were no official statistics on discrimination or violence based on sexual orientation or gender identity, there were reports of such discrimination. Representatives of international and local organizations reported that negative social attitudes towards marginalized groups, including LGBT persons, impeded these groups' willingness to come forward, organize, or seek access to HIV/AIDS programs.

LGBT individuals, particularly gay men, were among the most oppressed groups, although the country does not outlaw consensual same-sex sexual activity. According to a 2009 Soros Foundation study, 64.1 percent of LGBT respondents said they did not face open discrimination in the workplace, although LGBT individuals often concealed their sexual orientation to avoid such discrimination. LGBT individuals whose sexual orientation became known publicly risked physical and verbal abuse, possible loss of employment, and unwanted attention from police and authorities. A local NGO working on LGBT issues noted that new regulations made gender reassignment more cumbersome but cited a slight improvement in public awareness of LGBT rights. Several LGBT organizations operating in the country reported that government-run HIV clinics occasionally breached confidentiality and reported patients' sexual orientation to their families and employers. The NGO Amulet reported that since the beginning of 2011 there were 16 attempts on the lives of LGBT persons and 298 cases of physical violence of varying degrees. There were 13 instances of LGBT persons being dismissed from work based on their sexuality, and two cases of landlords refusing to rent property to LGBT persons. The organization reported 115 cases of LGBT persons being denied the right to health care.

According to one NGO working on LGBT issues, in December a transgender person shared some of the challenges facing the LGBT community with the television program "Drugaya Pravda" that aired on the national channel KTK. When the program was aired, the presenter described him as gay and presented the information he gave in a negative light. After receiving numerous threats, the person's house was burned down. The victim appealed to police, who were investigating the situation. The victim believed the incident was related to his admission of being transgender.

NGOs reported that members of the LGBT community seldom turned to law enforcement agencies to report violence against them, because they feared they would be met with hostility, ridicule, and occasionally violence. Additionally they did not want law enforcement officers to notify their employers of their sexual orientation.

Other Societal Violence or Discrimination

The law prohibits discrimination against persons with HIV and AIDS. Observers reported that cultural stigmas against drug users and other at-risk groups continued to affect general access to information, services, treatment, and care.

Section 7. Worker Rights

a. Freedom of Association and the Right to Collective Bargaining

The law and related regulations protect the right of workers to form and join independent unions, and bargain collectively. The law likewise protects the right of workers to form and join independent unions and bargain collectively.

The law protects workers' right to bargain collectively and negotiate collective agreements. Labor law provides that an individual contract between an employer and each employee sets the employee's wage and outlines the rights and responsibilities of the employee and the employer. The International Labor Organization observed that the country's labor code allows nonunion elected representatives to participate in collective bargaining in a way that could undermine the position of labor unions.

The law protects the right of workers to strike, but exercising this right is subject to numerous legal limitations. The law limits the conditions under which workers in certain professions that provide essential services, such as railway, civil aviation, military, law enforcement, fire services, and health, can strike. In general the law protects the right of workers to strike only if a labor dispute has not been resolved through existing compulsory arbitration procedures. Decisions to strike must be taken in a meeting where at least half of workers are present. Striking workers must give five days' advance notice to employers. The law neither sanctions nor prohibits the firing of employees for participation in an illegal strike.

The Law on Public Associations requires a minimum of 10 persons to establish a labor union. To obtain legal status, a trade union must apply for registration with the Ministry of Justice. The registration procedure is broadly similar to that of other membership organizations.

Foreign workers have the right to join unions; however, the law prohibits the operation of foreign unions and prohibits the financing of unions by foreign legal entities and citizens, foreign states, and international organizations. The law prohibits antiunion discrimination, and a court can order a worker reinstated if the court found the worker was fired for union activity.

In practice the government continued to restrict the right to organize, and most workers were not able to join or form trade unions of their choice. The government exercised considerable influence on organized labor and favored state-affiliated unions over independent unions. The largest trade union association, the Federation of Trade Unions, the successor to formerly state-sponsored Soviet-era labor organizations, remained affiliated with the government. The federation unites 26 industrial national unions and 13 regional unions. The industrial unions represented workers in a wide range of industries, including oil and gas, construction, textiles, education, and public health. Each union elects its own leader and has a representative on the

General Council, which elects the 14- member Executive Committee. The committee runs the federation's day-to-day operations and deals with issues of social and economic protection, labor protection, organization, and international cooperation.

Union demands that management finds unacceptable may be presented to a tripartite commission composed of government, employer association, and labor union representatives. Both state-affiliated and independent labor unions participate in tripartite commissions. The government was supposed to be the neutral broker on the commissions, but there were cases in which it favored the interests of labor unions or employers. The tripartite commission is responsible for developing and signing annual agreements governing most aspects of labor relations. Through this mechanism, labor unions raised the minimum wage for several industries, including mining and metallurgy, and employers were required to pay back salaries in a number of industrial areas during the year. Employers occasionally used individual contracts to weaken collective bargaining power. Activists stressed that political pressure on employers to avoid prolonged strikes following the violence in Zhanaozen was driving the rapid conclusion of agreements.

In practice there were reports of employers providing arbitrary justifications for firing employees who had attempted to organize strikes and there were multiple violations of the law protecting workers from antiunion discrimination. The violations ranged from threats of being fired, which would lead to the loss of social benefits, to physical intimidation and assault. Activists and trade union leaders in a variety of sectors became victims of these firings, harassment campaigns, and physical attacks. According to activists, the government did not interfere with the formation and operation of independent labor unions. There were reports of employers trying to neutralize the activity of independent labor unions by creating "yellow unions" with which to negotiate and sign collective bargaining agreements.

The leader of Independent Labor Unions asserted some provisions of the collective bargaining agreement with PetroKazakhstan violated the rights of employees. At year's end there was no information about the resolution of the conflict. The independent labor union For Decent Labor was unable to reach a collective bargaining agreement with EuroTechService. The company then negotiated and quickly signed an agreement with a newly formed union. For Decent Labor filed a complaint with the local labor department, which ordered EuroTechService to resume negotiations with the independent union. At year's end negotiations continued.

On December 28, approximately 70 public sanitation contractors at a public utility company in the western city of Aktau staged an unsanctioned rally in response to rumors of pending layoffs and low wages. After regional government representatives pledged to address their concerns, the protesters disbanded.

b. Prohibition of Forced or Compulsory Labor

The law prohibits all forms of forced or compulsory labor, except at the sentence of the court or in conditions of a state of emergency or martial law; however, there were reports that such practices occurred. The government conducted joint-agency operations to find victims of forced labor and trafficking, but victim identification remained weak.

There were reports that some employers abused both male and female migrant workers by confiscating their passports or using debt bondage, violence, or threats of violence to compel them to work. Reports varied on the exact number of labor migrants in the country. Estimates ranged from 300,000 to one million, with the majority of migrant workers coming from Kyrgyzstan, Tajikistan, and Uzbekistan. Migrant workers were primarily employed in agriculture and construction. The Ministry of Labor and Social Protection was responsible for handling issues related to migrant labor.

Also see the Department of State's *Trafficking in Persons Report* at www.state/j/tip.

c. Prohibition of Child Labor and Minimum Age for Employment

The law protects children from exploitation in the workplace. The minimum age for employment is 16. With parental permission, children between 14 and 16 years of age can perform light work that does not interfere with their health or education. The law also restricts the length of the workday for employees younger than 18. During the year the government amended legislation to allow children of migrant workers access to schools, which was intended to reduce the risk of child labor within the migrant population. The government conducted labor inspections to enforce the minimum age for employment, but enforcement was insufficient due to the relatively small number of inspectors, restrictions on inspections, and weak victim identification.

The government approved a 2012-14 Joint Action Plan for the Elimination of the Worst Forms of Child Labor under which it conducted awareness campaigns and conferences. Nevertheless, NGOs contended that the government's efforts and resources dedicated to enforcement were insufficient to address fully the use of child labor.

The government concluded an agreement with national employer associations that committed them to eradicate the use of forced labor and the worst forms of child labor and to develop alternative employment opportunities for children and their families. However, NGOs contended that the government's efforts and resources dedicated to enforcement were insufficient to address fully the use of child labor.

The Ministry of Labor and Social Protection is responsible for enforcement of child labor laws and for administrative offenses punishable by fines. The MIA is responsible for investigating criminal offenses. During the year the government reported no crimes related to illegal child labor. The government cooperated with trade unions, employers, and NGOs to raise awareness and promote interagency cooperation in eliminating child labor.

Children, however, worked in agriculture, notably in tobacco and cotton, especially during the harvest season of the latter. Efforts by NGOs, the government, and Philip Morris Kazakhstan, the sole purchaser of Kazakhstani tobacco, to eradicate child labor in its supply chain drastically reduced the numbers of migrant children in the tobacco fields and led to increased awareness among farmers and local officials. Concurrently the government improved enforcement of legislation to prevent child participation in the cotton harvest.

Past NGO studies found that more than 70 percent of the children employed in agricultural work were from migrant families, primarily Uzbek and Kyrgyz. Labor conditions in cotton fields frequently presented a physical health risk, and some children suffered from inadequate rest and nutrition. Many child workers in cotton lacked proper clothing to protect them from harmful chemicals used in agriculture and harsh weather conditions. In urban areas the country's increasingly formalized labor market led to a decrease in many forms of child labor, although there were still reports of children begging, unloading freight, delivering goods in markets, washing cars, and working at gas stations.

Also see the Department of Labor's *Findings on the Worst Forms of Child Labor* at www.dol.gov/ilab/programs/ocft/tda.htm.

d. Acceptable Conditions of Work

The national monthly minimum wage was 17,439 tenge (approximately $116). Most workers earned above the minimum wage in urban areas. As of 2009, 8.2 percent of the population lived below the poverty line. According to the government, the poverty line was 40 percent of the subsistence level income and was 6,247 tenge ($41.65). The law does not require equal pay for equal work.

The law stipulates that the normal workweek should not exceed 40 hours and limits heavy manual labor or hazardous work to no more than 36 hours a week. The law limits overtime to two hours a day or one hour a day for heavy manual labor and requires overtime to be paid at least a 50 percent premium. The law prohibits compulsory overtime and overtime for work in hazardous conditions. The law provides that labor agreements may stipulate the length of working time, holidays, and paid annual leave for each worker. The government sets occupational health and safety standards. The law requires employers to suspend work that could endanger the life or health of workers and to warn workers about any harmful or dangerous work conditions or the possibility of any occupational disease. The law specifically grants workers the right to remove themselves from situations that endanger their health or safety without suffering adverse employment action.

The Ministry of Labor and Social Protection enforced minimum wages, workhour restrictions, overtime, and occupational safety and health standards. Ministry inspectors conducted random inspections of employers. The Ministry of Labor and Social Protection had 300 labor inspectors. Penalties were considered sufficient to deter violations, but the number of inspectors was not enough to cover all sectors and regions adequately.

Occupational safety and health conditions in the construction, industrial, agricultural, and industrial construction sectors were often substandard. Workers in factories usually lacked protective clothing and worked in conditions of poor visibility and ventilation.

Labor advocates also reported that some employers regularly violated these laws. There were reports that management ignored regulations concerning occupational health and safety. In the first 11 months of the year, the Ministry of Labor and Social Protection reported 15,824 inspections and 19,304 violations of occupational health and safety standards and rules. In addition to inspections by the ministry, unions conducted inspections of unionized enterprises and reported their findings to authorities for investigation.

Some workers, particularly in the construction industry, were not free to exercise the right to remove themselves from situations that endangered their health and safety without jeopardizing their employment. During the first nine months of the year the government reported 1,479 workplace injuries, compared with 2,179 during all of 2011. The government did not report on the number of workplace deaths during the year, but there were 365 workplace deaths in 2011. According to officials at the Federation of Trade Unions, many of the deaths were due to antiquated equipment, Soviet-era infrastructure, and disregard for safety regulations in the mining and metallurgy sectors. There were no major industrial accidents in which a significant number of workers were injured or killed.

In: Kazakhstan ISBN: 978-1-62948-356-6
Editors: R. M. Hoyt and M. B. Weston © 2013 Nova Science Publishers, Inc.

Chapter 3

KAZAKHSTAN 2012 INTERNATIONAL RELIGIOUS FREEDOM REPORT*

U.S. Department of State, Bureau of Democracy, Human Rights and Labor

EXECUTIVE SUMMARY

The constitution provides for religious freedom; however, other laws and policies restrict religious freedom and, in practice, the government generally enforced these restrictions. The government's respect for religious freedom did not change significantly during the year. The government generally respected the religious freedom of most registered religious groups; however, it enforced restrictions and harassed unregistered and minority religious groups, often through fines and raids. The government implemented a 2011 law applying stringent mandatory registration requirements on missionaries and religious groups. The law gives the government broad grounds to deny religious groups legal status. While most religious groups managed to obtain legal registration, some were denied registration because they lacked the requisite number of members, and a few groups, such as Scientologists, the Unification Church, and Ahmadi Muslims, were denied registration based on their religious beliefs. The Religious Affairs Agency's (RAA) very broad mandate provides the

---

* This is an edited, reformatted and augmented version of a U.S. Department of State, Bureau of Democracy, Human Rights and Labor publication, dated May 2013.

potential to restrict religious freedom further, and its rules seem to require all Muslim groups to register under the Hanafi Sunni Spiritual Administration of Muslims in Kazakhstan (SAMK).

There were reports of societal discrimination based on religious affiliation, belief, or practice. Muslim, Russian Orthodox, Roman Catholic, Lutheran, and Jewish leaders reported high levels of acceptance in society.

The ambassador and other U.S. officials engaged in extensive private and public dialogue with the government to urge that implementation of the 2011 law on religion be consistent with the country's constitutional provisions for religious freedom and with its international commitments.

Section I. Religious Demography

According to Agency of Statistics 2012 data, the population is 16.9 million. There are approximately 3,088 registered religious organizations in the country, representing 17 different confessions.

Approximately 65 percent of the population is Muslim; the majority is Sunni of the Hanafi school. Other Islamic groups that account for less than 1 percent of the population include Shafi'i Sunni, Shia, Sufi, and Ahmadi. The highest concentration of self-identified practicing Muslims is in the southern region bordering Uzbekistan.

Orthodox Christians constitute approximately 24.6 percent of the population. Other groups constituting less than 5 percent of the population include Roman Catholics, Greek Catholics, Jehovah's Witnesses, Lutherans, Presbyterians, Seventh-day Adventists, Methodists, Mennonites, the Church of Jesus Christ of Latter-day Saints (Mormons), Jews, Buddhists, Hare Krishnas, Bahais, Christian Scientists, Scientologists, and members of Grace Church, New Life Church, and the Unification Church.

Section II. Status of Government Respect for Religious Freedom Legal/Policy Framework

The constitution provides for religious freedom; however, other laws and policies restrict religious freedom. The constitution defines the country as a secular state and provides the right to decline religious affiliation.

The religion law passed in 2011 and implemented during the year narrows the constitutional legal provisions for religious freedom, including by instituting a more restrictive mandatory re-registration requirement, mandating a tiered hierarchy for religious groups, and providing for government inspection of religious literature and bans on religious ceremonies in government buildings, military, law enforcement, and secular education institutions.

According to the law, all existing religious groups had until October 24 to reregister with both the central government and local governments of individual regions (oblasts) in which they have congregations. To register locally, a religious group must submit an application listing the names and addresses of at least 50 founding members to the Ministry of Justice (MOJ). Communities may only practice within the geographic limits of the locality in which they register, unless they have sufficient numbers to register at the regional or national level. To register regionally, groups must have 500 members in each of two separate regions while national registration requires 5,000 members with sufficient representation in each of the country's oblasts. These requirements make it very difficult for smaller religious groups to register and impossible for any group other than the SAMK and the Russian Orthodox Church to register at the national level.

All registered mosques are affiliated with the SAMK, a national organization with extremely close ties to the government, which is headed by a chief mufti based in Almaty. Some of these groups choose to associate themselves with the SAMK to obtain registration. Those not affiliated with the SAMK, such as the Ahmadiyya Muslim Community, are denied registration.

The law allows everyone to follow his or her religious or other convictions, take part in religious activities, and disseminate their beliefs, with some restrictions. The law states that the government shall not interfere with the choice of religious beliefs or affiliation of citizens, foreigners, or persons without citizenship, or the rearing of their children consistent with their convictions unless such upbringing harms the child's health, infringes on the child's rights, or is directed against the country's constitutional framework, sovereignty and territorial integrity. The law bans forced conversion of persons into a religion, forced participation in a religious group's activities, or compelled religious rites. The law bans religious activities related to coercion of citizens, foreigners, or persons without citizenship, that harm their health, force them to end marriages or family relations, or harm their morale. The law bans religious groups that use various methods including charity, blackmail, violence or a threat of using violence, or material or other dependence to induce persons to engage in their activities. The law also bans unregistered missionary activity.

The law as written, without any accompanying implementing legislation, gives the government broad grounds to deny religious groups legal status. The government may deny registration based on an insufficient number of adherents or inconsistencies between the provisions of a religious group's charter and the law. Police, prosecutors, and citizens may petition a court to suspend the activities of a registered group for failure to rectify violations or for repeated violations of the law. The Administrative Code stipulates a three-month suspension for registered groups that hold illegal gatherings, disseminate unregistered religious materials, systemically pursue activities that contradict the charter and bylaws of the group as registered, construct religious facilities without a permit, or otherwise defy the constitution or laws. During a suspension, the group is prohibited from speaking with the media; holding meetings, gatherings, or services; and undertaking financial transactions other than continued contractual obligations, such as paying salaries. If a religious group engages in activities prohibited by law or fails to rectify violations that led to a suspension, the government bans the group.

The law also allows authorities to suspend the activities and fine the leaders of unregistered groups. If a religious group engages in illegal activity or fails to rectify violations resulting in a suspension, its leader is subject to a fine of 485,400 tenge ($3,302), or 809,000 tenge ($5,503) if the group is registered as a legal entity. If a group engages in activities not specified in its charter, its leaders are subject to fines of 323,600 tenge ($2,201), or 485,400 tenge ($3,302) if the group is registered as a legal entity. If a group holds gatherings or conducts charity activities in violation of the law; imports, publishes and/or disseminates illegal religious literature or other materials; or constructs an unregistered building, its leaders are subject to fines of 161,800 ($1,101) tenge or 323,600 tenge ($2,201) for legal entities.

The Religious Affairs Agency (RAA) is responsible for the formulation and implementation of state policy in the area of religious freedom. The agency also studies and analyzes the status of religion, the operation of religious groups, and the activities of missionaries. It drafts legislation and regulations, conducts analysis of religious materials, considers problems related to violations of the religion law, initiates proposals with law enforcement on banning the operation of religious groups or individuals who violate the religion law, coordinates actions of local government in regulation of religious problems, and provides official interpretation of the religion law.

In addition to the more stringent mandatory registration requirements, the broad scope of the law, and the wide authority given to the RAA, there were several cases involving harassment of religious groups and their members. There were several incidents in which RAA officials participated along with police in raids on religious communities.

The government enforced existing restrictions on unregistered groups and minority religious groups. Local officials attempted to limit, often through raids, the activities of some minority religious groups, including evangelical Christians, Jehovah's Witnesses, Scientologists, and Muslims not affiliated with the SAMK. The government applied laws governing unregistered religious groups unevenly during the year. Local and national law enforcement authorities prosecuted and fined so-called "nontraditional" religious groups for conducting illegal or unsanctioned educational, religious, or entrepreneurial activities.

During the year, government officials continued to express concern regarding the potential spread of "political and religious extremism." The Committee for National Security continued to characterize the fight against so-called "religious extremism" as a top priority of the internal intelligence service and to expand its monitoring of civil society and religious groups.

The authorities' alleged fear of "extremism" led to some reports of abuses. According to the Head of the Department for Combating Extremism, the Ministry of Interior (MOI) banned the activity of 60 unregistered religious groups during the year. Also, since 2010 the government has banned over 950 websites, citing "extremism."

Several government-controlled media outlets and government-funded nongovernmental organizations (NGOs) continued to publish or broadcast stories critical of minority religious groups including evangelical Protestant Christian groups such as the New Life Church and Grace Church, and Scientologists, depicting them as dangerous "sects" harmful to society.

The government continued to use property laws against the Ahmadi Muslim community. The Almaty Territorial Land Inspection Committee filed a case against the Ahmadi community for violating the Land Code and the Administrative Code. According to the claim, the Ahmadis were using residential property for commercial and religious purposes. The community was fined 48,540 tenge ($300), but the property was not seized.

The Baptist Council of Churches reported several administrative court cases against individual Baptists throughout the country for participating in the activities of an unregistered group. The council had a policy neither to seek nor accept registration in former Soviet countries, and church members criticized the intrusive nature of the registration process, which required information about ethnicity, family status, religious education, employment, and political affiliation.

During the year, the Protestant groups New Life Church, Grace Church, and the Baptist Council, along with several congregations of Jehovah's Witnesses and Scientologists, reported that the authorities had raided their groups, including registered groups.

Courts typically fined individuals found guilty of unregistered religious activity. The Baptist Council of Churches reported instances in which pastors were fined for unregistered religious activities and, on several occasions, local law enforcement representatives questioned group members in their homes. Council members usually refused to pay fines for non-registration.

In December an Almaty court issued a decision to ban the Azeri Fatimai Shia group after it was denied re-registration. The RAA reported that it denied registration because of improper documentation, but group members asserted that they were denied registration because they did not join the SAMK. The court put a lien on the group's property, valued at 45 million tenge ($300,000). The group's appeal was pending at year's end, and the lien on the property was stayed until a final judgment on the appeal.

At the conclusion of the re-registration process in late-October, authorities announced a significant decrease in the total number of registered religious groups. According to official sources, 32 percent of all previously registered religious groups were not re-registered. The number of legally recognized groups fell from 4,551 to 3,088. According to official sources, many of the deregistered groups no longer existed or did not have the 50 adult "founding members" required for re-registration. Many of these smaller groups chose to join together, at least on paper, to clear the 50 member hurdle for registration.

When authorities refused or significantly delayed registration, they usually claimed that a group did not have the requisite number of "founding members," or the group's charter did not meet the requirements of the law and needed to undergo an expert theological review. NGOs and religious communities suggested that such requirements were often invoked as a pretext for denying or delaying registration of groups the government did not wish to recognize. Members of some minority religious groups reported that authorities had pressured them to remove their signatures from the re-registration documents.

During the year, authorities denied registration to at least three religious groups based on their theological views. The RAA "expert analysis" determined that the Church of Scientology was a group primarily engaged in commercial activity, and subsequently denied registration to its two congregations. On December 6, a court in Almaty ordered the closure of the Almaty Church of Scientology, and on December 7, an Almaty court ordered the closure of the Medeo Church of Scientology. Both cases were under appeal. Authorities also denied registration to the Unification Church of Almaty on the grounds that the RAA "expert analysis" determined that it did not meet the definition of a religion. On November 27, an Almaty court ordered the church closed at the request of the Ministry of Justice. The Unification Church appealed the ruling and a hearing was pending at year's end. While most religious groups received registration by year's end, authorities denied registration to a few individual protestant churches, as well as the Unification Church and the Church of Scientology. Authorities denied the Ahmadiyya Muslim group registration on the basis that their theology differed from mainstream Islam, and they therefore were not considered Muslims.

Under the current re-registration requirements, all mosques were seemingly required to join the SAMK in order to obtain legal registration. At year's end, there remained a few independent Muslim groups still seeking religious registration, such as the Tatar-Bashkir Din-Mohammad Mosque in Petropavl, and a few continued without religious registration. The SAMK exercised significant influence over the activities of Muslim groups, including mosque construction, imam appointments, and the administration of examinations and background checks for aspiring imams. The SAMK was the primary coordinator of Hajj travel and authorized travel agencies to provide Hajj travel services to citizens.

The law's vague definition of missionary activity allowed the authorities to interpret religious activity by visiting foreigners as missionary activity and expel those who were not registered as missionaries. The MOI reported that it identified 67 unregistered missionaries, including 13 foreigners, operating during the year. Of the foreign missionaries, five were deported, two were fined 184,000 tenge ($1,200) each, and six were given warnings.

On December 4, the Astana Administrative Court convicted Dmitry Bukin of unregistered missionary activity and fined him 161,900 tenge ($1,074), after Bukin organized a September 15-16 religious convention at a rented location in Astana. The Astana city prosecutor's office determined that Bukin unlawfully engaged in "missionary activity" by arranging the convention, attended by approximately 200 people, many of whom were Jehovah's Witnesses, and participating in the program as one of the speakers.

SECTION III. STATUS OF SOCIETAL RESPECT FOR RELIGIOUS FREEDOM

There were reports of societal discrimination based on religious affiliation, belief, or practice. Observers noted increased discrimination against religious minorities. The government-funded "Centers for Support to Victims of Destructive Sects" portrayed some minority religious groups as harmful. Some minority religious groups complained that members of these Centers disrupted their services or attempted to intimidate parishioners through threats of legal action. Scientologists reported that local businesses in Almaty frequently refused to rent them space to hold gatherings.

Some individuals reported being wary of minority religious groups, particularly those which proselytized. There were several reports of citizens filing complaints with authorities after their family members became involved with such groups.

Leaders of the five religious groups the government considered "traditional" -- Islam (as represented by the SAMK), Russian Orthodoxy, Roman Catholicism, Lutheranism, and Judaism -- reported general acceptance and tolerance that other minority religious groups did not always enjoy.

SECTION IV. U.S. GOVERNMENT POLICY

In discussions with government officials and in public statements, U.S. officials emphasized the importance of respecting human rights, and noted that bilateral cooperation on economic and security matters is a complement to, not a substitute for, meaningful progress on human rights, including religious freedom.

The ambassador, embassy officers, and other U.S. government officials remained engaged in dialogue with the government to seek assurance that implementation of the 2011 religion law was consistent with the country's constitutional provisions and international commitments to respect individuals' rights to peaceful expression of religious beliefs. U.S. officials expressed concern that the new law would not permit the registration of small religious groups and that its broad scope could enable authorities to apply it in an arbitrary manner.

Embassy and Department of State officials visited houses of worship in several regions of the country, met with religious leaders, and requested that government officials address specific cases of concern.

The U.S. embassy also maintained contact with a wide range of religious communities and religious freedom advocates, and reported on violations of their constitutional and human rights. Senior U.S. government officials met with senior government officials and members of religious groups to raise concerns over the 2011 religion law and its implementation, and senior U.S. government officials participated in high-level discussions on religious tolerance during the country's chairmanship of the Organization for Islamic Cooperation.

In addition, U.S. embassy officials attended public events in support of religious communities and participated in roundtables and other public debates on matters of religious freedom and tolerance. U.S. government representatives were in regular contact with NGOs that followed religious freedom topics, including the Almaty Helsinki Committee, the Association of Religious Organizations of Kazakhstan, and the Kazakhstan Bureau of International Human Rights and Rule of Law.

In: Kazakhstan ISBN: 978-1-62948-356-6
Editors: R. M. Hoyt and M. B. Weston © 2013 Nova Science Publishers, Inc.

Chapter 4

2013 Investment Climate Statement: Kazahstan*

Bureau of Economic and Business Affairs

Openness to, and Restrictions upon, Foreign Investment

Kazakhstan has made significant progress toward the creation of a market economy since it gained independence in 1991, and the European Union (2000) and the U.S. Department of Commerce (March 2002) have granted it market economy status. Kazakhstan also has attracted significant foreign investment since independence. As of September 30 2012, foreign investors had placed a total of $177.7 billion in Kazakhstan, primarily in the oil and gas sector. Kazakhstan is widely considered to have the best investment climate in the region. Numerous international firms have established regional headquarters in Kazakhstan.

The government's Program for Accelerated Industrial Development, part of its "Road Map for Business 2020," created investment priorities aimed at diversifying Kazakhstan's economy away from an overdependence on extractive industries. The government of Kazakhstan adopted a "National Plan for Attracting Investment" in December 2011 which seeks to improve the

* This is an edited, reformatted and augmented version of a Bureau of Economic and Business Affairs publication, dated February 2013.

investment climate by simplifying visa procedures, customs clearance, and transit across borders, as well as establishing special service centers for foreign investors under regional municipal authorities. In 2012, every regional government set up an Investors' Service Center.

In 2011, Kazakhstan announced the goal of joining the Organization of Economic Cooperation and Development (OECD). To meet OECD requirements, the government will need to amend its investment legislation.

Kazakhstan submitted its Memorandum on the Foreign Trade Regime (MFTR) to the World Trade Organization (WTO) in 1996 and the first round of consultations on accession took place in 1997. Kazakhstan has made significant progress in implementing the legal framework necessary for WTO accession and has signed bilateral protocols on market access for goods and services with the bulk of working party members. Multiparty talks have been more contentious with difficult negotiations centering on agricultural subsidies, sanitary and phytosanitary standards, local content requirements, export duties on petroleum, and enforcing intellectual property rights for pharmaceuticals. Despite domestic opposition to compromising on these issues, the government has vowed to satisfy working party concerns by the middle of 2013 in order to accede to the WTO by the end of the year.

Russia, Belarus, and Kazakhstan officially entered into a Customs Union on July 1, 2010. As a condition of membership, Kazakhstan has almost doubled its average import tariff and introduced annual tariff-rate quotas (TRQs) on poultry, beef, and pork. U.S. exporters have raised concerns about the possible trade-limiting effects of these TRQs, as well as the way TRQs are calculated and distributed. According to the Ministry of Economic Development and Trade, Kazakhstan will slightly increase tariff rate quotas in 2013.

On January 1, 2012, the Customs Union partners created the Common Economic Space (CES) which is intended to be a step toward further economic integration. While many agreements for the Common Economic Space are still being negotiated, the first 17 came into force in 2012. The government of Kazakhstan has asserted that CES agreements comply with WTO standards. If CES agreements are not WTO compliant, however, WTO commitments supersede CES rules.

The following acts of legislation impact foreign investment in Kazakhstan: 1) the 2003 Law on Investments; 2) the 2003 Customs Code and the Customs Code of the Customs Union, which came into force in July 2010; 3) the Tax Code; 4) the Law on Currency Regulation and Currency control; and 5) the Law on Government Procurement. These laws provide for non-expropriation, currency convertibility, guarantees of legal stability, transparent government procurement, and incentives for priority sectors. Inconsistent implementation of these laws and regulations at all levels of the government, combined with a tendency for courts to automatically accept government positions, can create significant obstacles to business in Kazakhstan.

The 2003 Law on Investments established a single investment regime for domestic and foreign investors and provides, inter alia, national treatment and non-discrimination for foreign investors. It guaranteed the stability of existing contracts at the time of its passage, with the qualification that new contracts will be subject to amendments in domestic legislation, certain provisions of international treaties, and domestic laws dealing with "national and ecological security, health, and ethics." The Law on Investments contains incentives and preferences for government-determined priority sectors, providing customs duty exemptions and in-kind grants (see Performance Requirements and Incentives). The Law also provides for dispute settlement through negotiation, Kazakhstan's judicial process, and international arbitration (see Dispute Settlement). In general, U.S. investors have expressed concerns about the Law's narrow definition of investment disputes, its lack of clear provisions for access to international arbitration, and certain aspects of investment contract stability guarantees.

In January 2009, Kazakhstan adopted a new Tax Code that lowered corporate income and value-added taxes, replaced royalty payments with a mineral extraction tax, and introduced excess profits and rent taxes on the export of crude oil and natural gas. Accordingly, the corporate income tax rate has dropped from 30% to 20%. The value-added tax (VAT) has been reduced gradually from 16% in 2006 to 12% in 2009 where it now remains and will likely remain in the near term. Kazakhstan applies a flat 11% social tax to employers based on employees' earnings and a personal income tax rate of 10%. The tax rate for non-residents is between 5% and 20%, depending on an individual's type of income. Subsurface users are subject to additional taxes: a signing bonus, commercial discovery bonus, and historical cost reimbursement.

Experts consider Kazakhstan's tax laws among the most comprehensive in the former Soviet Union. It is common for Kazakhstan's tax authorities to invoke the national Tax Code provisions over International Financial Reporting Standards (IFRS). At times this can lead to double taxation, especially when employing IFRS standards for deducting expenses between a company's home office and its branch office in Kazakhstan (see Dispute Settlement).

In 2001, Kazakhstan adopted transfer pricing legislation which gives tax and customs officials the authority to monitor export-import transactions. A transfer pricing law that came into force on January 1, 2009, introduced the commonly accepted "arm's length principle" embraced by the OECD. The law was amended in 2010 to provide for rights and liabilities of government agencies, the right of a transaction party to provide state agencies with a justification for applied prices, and the right to appeal results of tax inspections. According to the law, the Ministry of Finance has the right to monitor transactions of companies by surveying the prices of transactions and analyzing companies' reports. Foreign investors concede that the new law is more closely aligned with international standards, but are concerned that the law will be applied not only to transactions with related parties, but to all international transactions. The Embassy is not aware of any cases involving the inappropriate application of transfer-pricing legislation in 2012.

Although no sectors of the economy are legally closed to investors, restrictions exist, such as a 20% ceiling on foreign ownership of media outlets and a 49% limit for foreign ownership in the telecommunications sector, which does not apply to mobile operators. The government has indicated that the restriction in the telecommunications sector will be removed following Kazakhstan's accession to the World Trade Organization (WTO). No constraints on the participation of foreign capital in the banking and insurance sectors exist, but there is a ban on foreign bank and insurance company branches operating in Kazakhstan. Foreign companies in the banking and insurance sector may instead form a local joint stock company under parent company ownership. Restrictions also exist on foreign ownership of land in Kazakhstan (see Right to Private Ownership and Establishment).

Foreign investors have complained about irregular application of laws and regulations, and have interpreted regulatory pressure as an effort to extract bribes. Some investors report harassment by the Financial Police via unannounced audits, inspections, and other methods. At times, the authorities have used criminal charges in civil disputes as a pressure tactic.

By law and in practice, foreign investors can participate in privatization projects. Many foreign companies, however, cite the need to defend their investments from a steady stream of decrees and legislative changes, most of which do not "grandfather" existing investments. Foreign investors also complain about arbitrary tax inspections, as well as problems in finalizing contracts, delays and irregular practices in licensing, and land fees. Foreign companies report that local authorities arbitrarily impose environmental fines which are then placed in the general budget vice being used to offset any alleged environmental damage. The national and local budgets include revenue from environmental fines, which can result in fines being levied to generate additional revenue, regardless of whether environmental regulations are breached or not. Some foreign firms have expressed concern about the failure of government organizations to fulfill their contractual obligations, particularly regarding payments, which can prevent the foreign partner from advancing its investment program. Investors can then be exposed to government charges of non-performance, which could allow the government to cancel the contract.

The government regulates foreign labor at macro and micro levels. Foreign workers must obtain work permits, which can be difficult and expensive. The government limits the issuance of work permits to boost local employment based on the area of specialization and geographic region. From 2003-2008, the quota for foreign labor steadily increased from 0.14% to 1.6% of the total workforce, but was reduced by half on the heels of the economic crisis in 2008. A foreign labor quota of 0.75% of the active labor force remained in force throughout 2009 and 2010, and was slightly increased in 2011 to 0.85%, reaching 1% in 2012. In 2013, the foreign labor quota is scheduled to grow to 1.2% of the active labor force.

A February 2011 amendment to Kazakhstan's Expatriate Workforce Quota and Work Permit Rules mandated that medium and large businesses have 90% local content in their workforce for technical personnel and 70% for company executives as of January 2012. Following a concerted campaign led by Western oil companies, Kazakhstan passed an October 2011 decree that exempts Kazakhstan's three largest hydrocarbon projects – Tengiz, Karachaganak and Kashagan – from the requirement for three years. Other foreign businesses find it difficult to meet the local content demands, especially in technical fields where Kazakhstan cannot supply skilled workers in sufficient numbers.

Index	Ranking	Year
Transparency International	133 (score:28)	2012
Heritage Economic Freedom	68(score: 63)	2013
World Bank Doing Business Report	49	2013

The 2011 law on migration allows foreign citizens with Kazakhstani residence permits to work in Kazakhstan without additional permission and without being counted against labor quotas. Kazakhstan also opened its labor market for its Common Economic Space partners Russia and Belarus. On

January 1, 2012, Kazakhstan cancelled labor quotas for citizens of Russia and Belarus, and labor migrants from those countries are able to stay in the country for 90 days without registration with the migration police

Foreign Investment in the Extractive Industries

Despite growing investment in Kazakhstan's energy sector, concerns remain about the government's tendency to challenge contractual rights, to legislate preferences for domestic companies, and to create mechanisms for government intervention in foreign companies' operations, particularly in procurement decisions. Together with vague and contradictory legal provisions that are often arbitrarily enforced, these negative tendencies feed a perception that Kazakhstan is a suboptimal investment environment.

Business associations and investment advisors are concerned that Kazakhstan's Tax Code could undermine tax stability clauses in existing and future subsoil contracts. The government has stated that it will only guarantee tax stability for existing production sharing agreements (PSAs) and for the one major hydrocarbon project that has a tax and royalty contract (Tengiz). Furthermore, in December 2011, the Minister of Finance publicly stated that only tax rates, but not tax filing/collection procedures, will be held stable. Contracts for Tengiz, Kashagan, and Karachaganak include tax stability clauses that theoretically shelter the operating companies from changes to the tax code or customs regime.

In April 2008, Kazakhstan introduced a customs duty on crude oil and gas condensate exports. The government zeroed the customs duty rate in January 2009, but then it re-introduced it at a rate of $20 a ton in August 2010. The customs duty doubled to $40 a ton as of January 1, 2011 and has not changed since. Companies that pay "rent tax," a tax on mineral/crude oil exports, are exempted from the customs duty on crude exports.

The government’s "local content" strategy is considered to have a discriminatory effect on foreign investors. International oil companies complain that implementation is uneven, irregular, and non-transparent, particularly at local levels of government. Representatives of international service companies also report that it is difficult to obtain Kazakhstani certificates of origin. According to the Local Content Law, a product must carry a certificate of origin issued in Kazakhstan to meet the local content criteria.

The 2010 Law on Subsoil and Subsoil Use contains explicit requirements regarding the purchase of local goods and services for all investments in offshore oil and gas exploration and production. A December 2009 Local Content Law also requires that companies set a minimum percentage of local content for goods and services in contracts, but does not articulate how to address existing contracts without such quotas. U.S. businesses have privately reported intense pressure from the government of Kazakhstan to rewrite contracts to meet the revised local content standards. The Local Content Law allows the state to revoke the subsoil production rights of companies that do not meet local content requirements during a project's exploration phase. The National Agency for Local Content Development (NALCD), under the Ministry of Industry and New Technologies, oversees local content policy. In April 2012, NALCD accused 38 mining companies of violating local content regulations (i.e. failure to provide information on planned and actual purchases of goods, works, and services in March 2012). The Agency threatened to impose penalties, including unilateral termination of subsoil use contracts; however, no contracts have thus far been annulled.

The government, led by the Ministry of Industry and New Technologies, is currently drafting an Action Plan on Enhancement of Local Content in Procurements for Major Subsoil Users and Strategic Mining and Petroleum Companies, which is scheduled for submission to the Presidential Administration in the first quarter of 2013. The Action Plan would require companies to utilize local content for 50% of Front End Engineering Design (FEED) and design works, would ban export of geological information (core samples, rocks and reservoir fluids) and would require the nomination of a Ministry of Industry and New Technologies representative onto Boards of Directors of key subsoil use projects. Kazakhstan's Foreign Investors Council has been given a draft of the Action Plan and provided comments outlining industry's concerns.

The Subsoil Law also allows the government to unilaterally amend existing contracts of "strategic significance" or even to terminate contracts deemed to threaten Kazakhstan's economic security or national interests. In April 2012, the government issued a new decree that enlisted 361 hydrocarbon fields and mineral deposits as having "strategic significance." Companies must also obtain the government's permission to conclude combined exploration and production contracts. Additionally, the Subsoil Law shortens the time limits for exploration contracts, enhances the government's authority to terminate contracts not in compliance with the law, requires parliamentary approval for tax stability clauses in individual contracts, and precludes the use of production sharing agreements (PSAs) in the future. Moreover, the Law treats draft work plans containing cost and production volume projections as formal contract commitments. Companies must establish equal terms, conditions, and pay for Kazakhstani and foreign workers, and the government should evaluate subsurface resource bids based on proposed social contributions. The Law also severely reduces gas flaring quotas and imposes harsher penalties for environmental violations.

The Subsoil Law reaffirms the state's preemptive right to participate in equity transactions involving subsurface user rights in oil and gas or mining operations, including but not limited to the purchase of shares in new exploration and production projects. The government can also block the sale of oil and gas assets and exclude specific companies from participating in oil and gas tenders in the interests of "national security." The Subsoil Law establishes transparent procedures for state and private companies to exercise subsurface rights, and clearly defines when the state can exercise its priority right. A December 2010 regulation established an interdepartmental committee to advise whether and how to exercise the government's preemptive rights in extractive projects.

On January 9, 2012, President Nazarbayev signed the Law on Natural Gas and Gas Supply. The Law aims to regulate gas transportation, distribution, and pricing, as well as to create a single, monopolistic operator to purchase natural gas. On July 5, 2012, Kazakhstan's state owned firm KazTransGaz was designated as the national gas operator.

CONVERSION AND TRANSFER POLICIES

In 1999, the government and National Bank of Kazakhstan announced that the national currency would be allowed to float freely at market rates. After a February 2009 tenge devaluation, the National Bank returned to a managed float exchange rate regime and maintained an exchange rate in the corridor 150 tenge/per U.S. dollar plus/minus 3%. In 2010, the National Bank broadened the corridor of fluctuation, allowing the tenge to float between 127.5 and 165 to the dollar. Although the National Bank cancelled the corridor of fluctuation and announced a return to a managed float exchange rate regime early in 2011, the exchange rate has not changed sharply. In 2012, the tenge fluctuated between 147.79 and 150.52 to the dollar.

In 1996, Kazakhstan adopted Article 8 of the IMF Articles of Agreement, which stipulates that current account transactions, such as currency conversions or the repatriation of investment profits, will not be restricted. No distinction is made between residents and non-residents in opening bank accounts, but all account holders must have a Kazakhstani tax identification number. Money transfers associated with foreign investments, whether inside or outside of the country, are unrestricted. Non-residents may be paid wages in a foreign currency (see Article 16 of the Law on Currency Regulation and Currency Control), and foreign investors may convert and repatriate earnings.

In June 2005, President Nazarbayev signed the Law on Currency Regulation and Currency Control. This law lifted restrictions on money transfers and allows individuals to take up to $10,000 in cash out of the country without documentation of the money's origin. The Russia- Belarus-Kazakhstan Customs Union further liberalized the money transfer regime by removing the requirement for a National Bank to certify money's origin in amounts over $10,000. On January 1, 2007, Kazakhstan eliminated all licensing requirements and procedures for foreign currency operations, except the licensing of foreign exchange operations. Banks conducting transactions in foreign currency, including bank payments and transfers relating to capital movements, must notify the National Bank of their operations as soon operations exceed a certain threshold. The notification threshold for capital outflow operations is $100,000 and for capital inflow operations is $500,000.

Export-import credits and financial loans with terms longer than 180 days fall under the National Bank's registration regime. Banks processing these credit transactions must register them and notify the National Bank before completing the transaction. Legislation stipulates that non-fulfillment of payment obligations on export of investment contracts triggers administrative or criminal charges. Administrative penalties are applied for non-payment of up to $50,000, above which criminal charges are applied.

The Law on Currency Regulation and Currency Control specified measures for a "special currency regime" which can only be introduced when the country's economic and financial stability are in jeopardy. Measures may include requirements for companies to retain a certain percentage of their foreign currency profits in the National Bank of Kazakhstan or other authorized banks, the mandatory sale of foreign currency earnings, and limits on the use of foreign bank accounts. Considered an extreme measure, its application in the foreseeable future appears unlikely.

The National Bank no longer requires so-called transaction passports for export-import operations following December 2011 legislative amendments to the Law on Currency Regulation and Currency Control. The law was simplified to instead require commercial banks to issue a contract registration number for imports and exports. A registration number is required for all transactions exceeding $50,000, and the procedure to receive a registration number can take several days.

The National Bank regularly monitors the currency operations of selected non-residents. This procedure primarily affects the oil and gas, construction, and mining industries, as well as companies providing architectural, engineering, and industrial design services. According to the National Bank, this monitoring provides better statistical data on the balance of payments and external debt. The U.S. Embassy is not aware of any concerns with regard to remittance policies or the availability of foreign exchange conversion for remittance of profits. However, Kazakhstan's 2012 Law on Electricity Generation could, in theory, be used to force electricity generators to reinvest all of their profits into infrastructure upgrades, thereby negating foreign investors' opportunity to realize profits or take them out of the country.

Expropriation and Compensation

The 2003 Law on Investments allows nationalization by the state in emergency cases "as provided in legislative acts of the Republic of Kazakhstan." Unlike its predecessor -- the 1994 Investment Law -- it does not provide clear grounds for expropriation, nor does it require "prompt, adequate and effective" compensation at a fair market value. The 2003 Law differentiates between nationalization and requisition, providing full indemnification in the case of the former, as opposed to payment of market value in the case of the latter. Bilateral investment treaties (BITs) between Kazakhstan and other countries, including the United States, require compensation in the event of expropriation.

There has been only one case of legal expropriation of a foreign investor's property for public purpose. The investor ultimately submitted the case for international arbitration and the government paid the amount awarded by the arbiter in May 2006.

Dispute Settlement

There have been a number of investment disputes involving foreign companies in the past several years. While the disputes have arisen from unrelated, independent circumstances, many are linked to alleged violations of environmental regulations, tax laws, transfer pricing laws, and investment clauses. Some disputes relate to alleged illegal extensions of the exploration schedule by subsurface users as costs incurred during this period are fully reimbursed under the terms of a production sharing agreement. In some instances, disputes involve hundreds of millions of dollars. Problems arise in the enforcement of judgments, and ample opportunity exists for influencing judicial outcomes given the relative lack of judicial independence.

Kazakhstan's Civil Code establishes general commercial law principles. The 2003 Law on Investments defines an investment dispute as "a dispute ensuing from the contractual obligations between investors and state bodies in connection with investment activities of the investor." It states that such disputes can be settled by negotiation, in Kazakhstani courts, or through international arbitration. According to the Law, disputes not falling within the aforementioned category "shall be resolved in accordance with the laws of the Republic of Kazakhstan." While the laws of Kazakhstan favor use of the Kazakhstani judicial system, when contracts include an international arbitration clause it is honored. Moreover, in 2004 Kazakhstan adopted a law on international arbitration.

Kazakhstan has been a member of the International Center for the Settlement of Investment Disputes (ICSID) since December 2001 and ratified the New York Convention on the Recognition and Enforcement of Foreign Arbitral Awards in 1995. By law, any international arbitral award rendered by the ICSID, a tribunal applying the UN Commission on International Trade Law Arbitration rules, Stockholm Chamber of Commerce, London Court of International Arbitration, or Arbitration Commission at the Kazakhstan Chamber of Commerce and Industry is enforceable in Kazakhstan.

Despite effective dispute resolution mechanisms for most commercial activity, an issue of serious concern for foreign investors is the lack of explicit provisions for international arbitration in the Subsoil Law. International law firms worry that because the Subsoil Law does not expressly provide for international arbitration, the government might choose not to include a provision in contracts to allow resolution of disputes through international arbitration. That said, in July 2010, then Prime Minister Karim Massimov ordered the Ministry of Justice to create a special legal department to defend the country's interests in international courts. Monetary judgments are normally made in domestic currency, but currency conversion is not a barrier to repatriation of awards.

Even when investment disputes are eventually resolved in accordance with contract conditions, the process of reaching a resolution can be very slow and involve considerable investment of time and resources. Many investors therefore elect to handle investment disputes privately, rather than make their cases public. The U.S. Embassy advocates on behalf of U.S. firms with investment disputes.

Additionally, the U.S. Ambassador participates in every meeting of the Prime Minister's Council to Improve the Investment Climate. The Council was created with the goal of paying special attention to questions related to foreign investors, including protection of their rights and interests. The Council proved to be an efficient forum for foreign companies to voice concerns about doing business in Kazakhstan in front of the country's Ministers and decision makers. In 2012, the Council discussed various issues, including tax administration problems, decriminalization of administrative violations, the rule of law, judicial independence, and the arbitrary application of environmental fines.

The 1997 Bankruptcy Law contains a detailed list of creditors' rights and prescribes mechanisms for enforcement. Amendments to the Law in 2008 provided a comprehensive list of the governmental authorities involved in bankruptcy procedures and expanded the rights of enterprises during rehabilitation procedures. According to Article 28 of the Civil Code, civil suits concerning the restructuring of financial institutions now fall within the jurisdiction of the Almaty Financial Court. The Court must approve creditor-agreed restructuring plans of financial institutions.

Performance Requirements and Incentives

The 2003 Law on Investments and 2008 Tax Code provide for tax preferences, customs duties exemptions, and in-kind grants as incentives for foreign and domestic investment in priority sectors. The Investment Committee under the Ministry of Industry and New Technologies makes decisions on customs duties exemptions (with notification to customs authorities) and in-kind grants on a case-by-case basis. The Investment Committee also ensures that investors meet their contractual obligations. The Law allows the government to rescind such incentives, collect back-payments, and/or revoke an investor's operating license if an investor fails to fulfill its contractual obligations. Tax preferences can be extended upon the decision of regional tax authorities.

The government uses preferences to help diversify its economy away from the extractive sector. Priority sectors include agriculture, construction, metallurgy, chemistry and pharmaceuticals, food production, consumer goods, oil refining, oil and gas infrastructure, metallurgy, transport, information communication, machinery, tourism, logistics, education, health care and aerospace. The system applies to new enterprises, as well as to existing enterprises making new investments. The duration of tax preferences increases with the size of investment.

In light of Kazakhstan's Accelerated Industrialization and Innovation Program (see Openness to, and restrictions upon, Foreign Investment), the government amended the Law on Investments in 2012 and broadened possible preferences to include "strategic investment projects." If the project helps develop the high-tech industry or exceeds $50 million of investment in an economically depressed region, it is eligible for property and land tax exemptions and/or subsidies for electricity and gas.

RIGHT TO PRIVATE OWNERSHIP AND ESTABLISHMENT

Private entities, both foreign and domestic, have the right to establish and own business enterprises, buy and sell business interests, and to engage in all forms of remunerative activity.

Kazakhstan's constitution provides that land and other natural resources may be owned or leased by Kazakhstani citizens in accordance with the law. The 2003 Land Code allows citizens of Kazakhstan (natural and legalized) and Kazakhstani companies to own agricultural and urban land, including commercial and non-commercial buildings, complexes, and dwellings thereupon situated. Amendments to the Labor Code in 2011 permit foreigners to own land to build industrial and non-industrial facilities, including dwellings. Foreigners may rent, but not own, agricultural land for up to 10 years. Foreigners may, however, own agricultural land through either a Kazakhstani-registered joint venture or a full subsidiary. The Land Law does not allow private ownership of the following types of land:

- land used for national defense and national security purposes;
- specially-protected natural territories;
- forests, reservoirs (lakes, rivers, canals, etc.), glaciers, swamps, etc.;
- public areas (urban or rural settlements);

- main railways and public roads;
- land reserved for future development and construction of national parks, railways and public roads, subsoil use and power facilities, and social infrastructure.

PROTECTION OF PROPERTY RIGHTS

Secured interests in property (fixed and non-fixed) are recognized under the Civil Code and the 2003 Land Code. All property and lease rights for real estate must be registered with the Ministry of Justice through its service centers distributed throughout the country.

Kazakhstan continues to move closer to international IPR standards. The Civil Code and various IPR laws, in principle, protect U.S. intellectual property. In 2006, USTR removed Kazakhstan from the Special 301 Watch list. In 2010, the government introduced amendments to trademark legislation that would bring provisions of the law in line with WTO guidelines for trade related aspects of intellectual property rights (TRIPS). Kazakhstan has also ratified 16 of the 24 treaties endorsed by the World Intellectual Property Organization (WIPO). In 2010, Kazakhstan joined the Madrid Agreement on the Repression of False or Deceptive Indications of Source on Goods and the Agreement Concerning the International Registration of Trademarks. It also ratified the Nairobi Treaty on the Protection of the Olympic Symbol. In 2011, Kazakhstan ratified the WIPO Patent Law Treaty.

In June 2011, Kazakhstan ratified the Agreement of the Common Economic Space on unified principles of regulation in the area of IPR protection. As follow-up steps within the framework of this agreement, in 2012 Kazakhstan ratified the Singapore Treaty on the Law of Trademarks and the Rome Convention for the Protection of Performers, Producers of Phonograms, and Broadcasting Organizations. In December 2011, Kazakhstan adopted amendments to IPR laws that enhance the responsibility for copyright violations on the internet and simplify procedures for trade mark registration.

Patent protection is available for inventions, industrial designs, prototypes, novel processes, and products that have industrial applications. The National Institute of Intellectual Property performs formal examinations of patent applications. Patents for inventions are granted for 20 years; patents for utility models are granted for a five year period with a possible three year extension. Prototypes patents are granted a 10 year initial period of protection, with the possibility of an additional five year extension. Kazakhstani legislation also permits an "innovation" patent, which is granted for an initial three year period with a possible extension for two years. Issued after only checking the local novelty of an invention, an innovation patent is expected to boost local business innovation. Unsuccessful applicants can appeal decisions of the National Institute of Intellectual Property and the Committee for Intellectual Property Rights. Kazakhstan is a member of the Moscow-based Eurasian Patent Bureau and the Munich-based European Patent Bureau.

Trademark violation is a crime in Kazakhstan. While trademarks are protected in Kazakhstan, counterfeit goods can be found at local markets. Registration fees charged to foreign patent and trademark applicants are significantly higher than those charged to domestic applicants. Applications for trademark, service mark, and appellations-of-origin protection should be filed with the National Patent Office and approved by the Committee for Intellectual Property Rights. Trademarks and service marks are afforded protection for 10 years from the date of filing. The Law on Copyrights and Related Rights was enacted in 1996. The law largely conforms to the requirements of the WTO TRIPS Agreement and the Berne Convention. One of the latest amendments to the Copyright Law allows licensed vendors to seek damages from unauthorized dealers selling pirated merchandise. Illegal software development and manufacture generally is not conducted in Kazakhstan. Russia, Ukraine and China are believed to be the local market's primary sources.

TRANSPARENCY OF THE REGULATORY SYSTEM

The non-transparent application of laws remains a major problem in Kazakhstan and an obstacle to expanded trade and investment. Foreign investors complain of inconsistent standards and corruption. While foreign participation in the economy is generally welcomed, some foreign investors point out that the government is not always evenhanded and sometimes reneges on its commitments. Although the Investment Committee of the Ministry of Industry and New Technologies was established to facilitate foreign investment overall, it has had limited success in addressing the concerns of foreign investors.

Kazakhstan has taken great strides to try to improve its business environment and streamline bureaucratic practices, including accelerating start-up procedures and reducing minimum capital requirements for businesses. The government also introduced new building regulations and a risk-based approach for permit approvals in 2009 to decrease the onerous nature of attaining construction permits. As a result, Kazakhstan moved up 15 places to 53 out of 183 countries in the World Bank's 2011 Doing Business Report. In 2012, Kazakhstan progressed to 47th place in the report's rankings. In the 2013 report, Kazakhstan placed 49th.

Kazakhstani law provides for government compensation for violations of contracts that were properly entered into and guaranteed by the government. However, where the government has merely "approved" or "confirmed" a foreign contract, the government's responsibility is limited to the performance of administrative acts (i.e., those "concerning the issuance of a license, granting of a land plot, mining allotment, etc.") necessary to facilitate a subject's investment activity. In those cases, commercial arbitration or other dispute resolution mechanisms would need to be used to redress contract violations.

A 2007 Licensing Law established the legal framework for licensing activities and simplified procedural requirements. The relevant agency must issue a license within one month of receiving the required documents from a company. Amendments to the law in 2012 require that all licenses be issued in electronic format. Toward this end, the government launched a special website (www.elicense.kz) which contains a license data base updated monthly. Despite the government's efforts to improve licensing procedures and reduce the number of licensed activities, the process remains time consuming, confusing, and costly, particularly for small-and-medium sized enterprises.

Efficient Capital Markets and Portfolio Investment

Kazakhstan has endeavored to create and implement a sound financial system and stable macroeconomic framework. As a result, the financial system has started to direct financial resources to the most promising parts of the economy. Official policy clearly supports credit allocation on market terms and the further development of legal, regulatory, and accounting systems consistent with international norms.

Most domestic borrowers obtain credit from Kazakhstani banks, although foreign investors find the bank margins and collateral requirements onerous. It is usually cheaper and simpler for foreign investors to use retained earnings or borrow from their home country. Since 1998, Kazakhstani banks have placed

Eurobonds on international markets and obtained syndicated loans to support domestic lending. Leading Kazakhstani banks were able to obtain reasonably good ratings from international credit assessment agencies until the global financial crisis struck. In operation since 1993, the Kazakhstani Stock Exchange (KSE) is an insignificant source of investment. Decreased capitalization and diminished transaction volumes at KSE have not impacted the overall economic situation or financial markets

In October 2008, the Kazakhstani government announced a stabilization plan in response to the global financial crisis that included a $10 billion bailout package for banks. In February 2009, the government, via parastatal holding company Samruk-Kazyna, acquired majority stakes in four systemically important banks: 75% of common shares in BTA, 100% of Alliance Bank, 20% of common shares in Halyk Bank, and 21% of common shares in KazKommertsBank. Early in 2011, Halyk Bank bought out its common shares from Samruk-Kazyn BTA, Alliance Bank, Astana Finance, and Temirbank all defaulted by the end of 2009 and began debt restructuring processes. BTA alone required over $16 billion in debt restructuring, while Alliance Bank had to negotiate $4.5 billion in additional debt. In 2010, Alliance Bank and BTA bank concluded debt restructuring negotiations.

At the end of December 2011, BTA bank announced the necessity of a second debt restructuring. BTA bank failed to make a $150 million coupon payment due on January 1, 2012. The restructuring plan was approved by creditors and the National Bank at the end of 2012. As a result, the debt of BTA bank will be reduced from $11 billion to approximately $3.3 billion. Samruk-Kazyna, which now owns 97% of BTA, has converted $1.2 billion of deposits into equity and will provide a $1.6 billion subordinated loan to the bank. Although the bank will be recapitalized and its equity will meet Basel II requirements, the bank is still recovering. Analysts consider BTA bank an outlier when assessing the overall health of the industry.

Kazakhstan has 38 commercial banks and as of November 1, 2012, the assets of the five largest banks, including KazKommertsBank, HalykBank, BTA bank, Bank CenterCredit and ATF-UniCredit bank were valued at 8.34 trillion tenge (approximately $55 billion).

Although stable, Kazakhstan's banking system has not yet recovered. The poor and deteriorating quality of many banking assets, capital constraints, and cautious lending policies remain major challenges. As of November1, 2012, the share of non-performing loans (NPL) remained a high 36%. Analysts noted, however, encouraging signs of recovery, including 10.5% loan growth from January through November 2012.

To help the banks deal with NPLs, the National Bank established a Distressed Assets Fund that became operational in summer 2012. As of September 2012, the fund's equity was around $33.5 million. Further capital injections from the National Bank will depend on the performance of the fund. The fund is expected to purchase from banks NPLs not backed by real estate. The National Bank also promulgated rules permitting commercial banks to create Special Purpose Vehicles (SPVs) for NPLs collateralized with real estate. As of January 2013, the two largest banks, Halyk Bank and KazKommertsBank, have created SPVs to address these types of bad loans.

Trading on the Kazakhstan Stock-Exchange (KSE) is dominated by block trades. The spreads are extremely wide, and the bulk of KSE trade is in foreign exchange which accounted for about 52% of total trade in 2012. Transactions with government securities accounted for 4.8% of KSE trade. In December 2012, the stock market capitalization of the KSE was $33.1 billion, and bond market capitalization was $40.5 billion. The number of listed companies dropped from 354 in 2010 to 122 in 2012.

In 2012, Samruk–Kazyna and KSE jointly launched the "People's IPO" designed to permit Kazakhstani citizens and entities to purchase stock in the country's state owned enterprises. The first stage of the program exceeded analysts' expectations when 34,000 individuals, 10 pension funds and one commercial bank purchased $393 million in shares of the parastatal pipeline company KazTransOil. The government and Samruk–Kazyna plan IPOs of other national companies, including KEGOC (operator of the electricity grid), KazMorTransFlot (a maritime shipping company), and eventually KazTransGas (the national gas operator) and Kazakhstan TemirZholy (the national railway company). Foreign companies and individuals will be eligible to purchase shares in these companies only on the secondary market.

Pension funds are investors in both the KSE and foreign markets. As of December 2012, 11 pension funds had accumulated 3,116.6 billion tenge (approximately $20.8 billion) in assets. According to national legislation, pension fund assets can only be invested in specific categories of securities, including corporate and government bonds, and securities issued by foreign governments and foreign corporations. The government is considering reform of the pension system, including a possible liberalization of the pension funds' investment rules and increasing the age of retirement for women.

There have been few hostile takeovers in Kazakhstan, probably because there are few publicly traded firms. Defensive measures against takeovers are not targeted toward foreign investors in particular. The Civil Code requires a company that has purchased a 20% share in another company to publish information about the purchase.

COMPETITION FROM STATE-OWNED ENTERPRISES

Officially, private enterprises compete with public enterprises under the same terms and conditions. However, state-owned enterprises generally enjoy better access to natural resources, markets, credit, and licenses than private entities.

The government of Kazakhstan has actively consolidated state-owned enterprises in recent years. At the end of 2012, six state-owned holding companies existed in Kazakhstan. Kazakhstani law requires national holding companies to publish annual reports and submit their books for independent audit. The following details each of the holding companies:

1. Samruk-Kazyna - National Welfare Fund (S-K) was modeled on Singapore's Temasek. Kazakhstan's largest national holding company, it manages the state's assets in oil and gas, energy, transportation, telecommunication, and the financial and innovation sectors. According to some estimates, Samruk-Kazyna controls more than half of Kazakhstan's economy and is the nation's largest buyer of goods and services. Samruk-Kazyna's official purpose is to facilitate economic diversification and to increase effective corporate governance; however, it spent its first two years spearheading the government's anti-financial crisis program.

   The Prime Minister chairs Samruk-Kazyna's Board of Directors, which includes the Ministers of Finance, Industry and Trade, Economic Development and Trade, and Oil and Gas, as well as the Head of the Presidential Administration (Chief of Staff) and three independent directors. In February 2009, President Nazarbayev signed a separate law providing Samruk-Kazyna special status and rights. Samruk-Kazyna can now conclude large transactions between members of its holdings without public notification. Samruk-Kazyna also has a pre-emptive right to buy strategic facilities and bankrupt assets. It is exempt from government procurement procedures and has the right to establish its own procurement rules. Moreover, the government can transfer to Samruk-Kazyna state-owned property, simplifying the process to transfer state property to private owners.

2. KazAgro manages the state's agricultural holdings, including the National Food Contract Corporation (government wheat purchasing agent), KazAgroFinance (equipment subsidy provider), Agrarian Credit Corporation, Corporation on Livestock Development, and the Fund for Financial Assistance to Agriculture. Chaired by one of the Deputy Prime Ministers, the Board of Directors includes the Ministers of Finance, Agriculture, and Economic Development and Trade, as well as three independent directors.
3. Parasat is charged with stimulating the development of scientific research and domestic capacity in the high-tech sector. The holding company manages several scientific institutions and funds. Chaired by one of the Deputy Prime Ministers, the Board includes the Minister of Education of Science, the Vice-Minister of Economic Development and Trade, the Chairmen of the State Property and Science Committees, and independent directors.
4. Zerde - National Informative and Communication Holding Company was created to develop modern information and communication technologies and to stimulate investments and innovations in the communication sector. The Managing Board's Chairman is subordinate to the Ministry of Communication and the Prime Minister's office.
5. The National Medical Holding company seeks to implement business-oriented and innovative corporate management in Astana's newly built medical facilities. In 2010, the holding company became a part of Nazarbayev University with the stated goal of creating favorable conditions for medical research and the use of advanced medical technologies in Astana. The Board of Directors is chaired by one of the Deputy Prime Ministers.
6. In 2011, the government established National Holding Company “Kasipkor” to develop a modern vocational education system in Kazakhstan in the areas of engineering, communication and information technologies, design, metallurgy, machinery building and crafts.

National Oil Fund

Kazakhstan has a sovereign wealth fund which is formally named the National Oil Fund of the Republic of Kazakhstan. Established by Presidential decree in 2000, the fund aims to diminish the country's budgetary dependence on fluctuating world oil prices and to accumulate savings to benefit future generations.

The Fund receives all direct taxes and a percentage of revenues from the oil sector, revenues from the privatization of state property in the mining and manufacturing industries, and proceeds from sales of farmlands, as well as the Fund's investment income. The Ministry of Finance owns the National Fund. The National Bank is its trustee, and selects external administrators from internationally recognized investment companies or banks to oversee the fund. Information on external administrators and the assets they manage is confidential.

In addition to preserving wealth for future generations, the Fund is also used to support the government's political and economic objectives. In February 2012, a $4 billion loan was extended from the Fund to Kazakhstan's state-owned oil company KazMunayGas (KMG) to support its participation in the Kashagan oil field. The National Fund also invests in the domestic economy through "official transfers to the state budget," which can now vary from $6.8 billion to $9.2 billion annually. President Nazarbayev has decreed that the National Fund should retain a minimum balance of no less than 20% of GDP.

In 2012, the National Bank founded the Investment Corporation to invest small portions of the National Fund and the Bank's international reserves in international markets in order to diversify Kazakhstan's assets and to increase its returns.

The Investment Corporation has been allotted $5 billion for the next five years to invest into private equity, hedge funds, real estate, and infrastructure projects abroad.

The Ministry of Finance and the National Bank prepare the National Fund's annual report, which the President approves. In addition, the Ministry of Finance and National Bank publish on their websites (www.minfin.kz, www.nationalbank.kz) monthly and annual reports on revenues and use of National Fund money.

Although these reports provide information on the Fund's general financial situation, they do not provide details. As of January 1, 2013, the National Fund's assets totaled $57.8 billion. Kazakhstan's total international reserves, including the National Bank's foreign currency and gold reserves, equaled $86.1 billion (in current prices).

Corporate Social Responsibility

Kazakhstan is in the process of adhering to OECD Guidelines for International Investment and Multinational Enterprises, and the government actively promotes the idea of corporate social responsibility. In his addresses to foreign investors and local businesses, President Nazarbayev has repeatedly asked them to implement corporate socially responsible projects, to provide occupational safety, to pay salaries on time, and to invest in human capital. The President annually awards "Paryz" ("Honors" in Kazakh) for achievements in corporate social responsibility.

Foreign Investors report that local government officials regularly pressure them to provide social investments in order to achieve local political objectives. These local officials also attempt exert as much control as possible over both the selection of and the subsequent allocation of funding for the projects.

Political Violence

There have been no incidents of politically motivated violence against foreign investment projects, and politically motivated civil disturbances remain exceptionally rare. In 2012, Kazakhstan experienced several incidents in which individuals or groups associated with Islamic extremists launched small-scale violent attacks against government offices, with most concentrating on police and national security organs. The violence has remained isolated and has not targeted foreign investment or foreigners working in Kazakhstan. Kazakhstan has good relations with its neighbors, although the government is concerned that the borders with Kyrgyzstan and Uzbekistan are vulnerable to penetration by extremist groups.

In the January 15, 2012 parliamentary elections, the president's party Nur Otan won 80 percent of the vote, Ak-Zhol won 7.47 percent, and the Communist People's Party won 7.19 percent. All three parties elected are generally considered supporters of President Nazarbayev. While the Organization for Security and Cooperation in Europe (OSCE) asserted that the election did not meet Kazakhstan's OSCE commitments or international standards for democratic elections, and opposition groups denounced the election as fraudulent, no significant demonstrations against the results occurred.

CORRUPTION

Although the Kazakhstani Criminal Code contains special penalties for accepting and giving bribes, corruption is common throughout Kazakhstan. The President issued an anti-corruption decree in April 2009 that provides whistle-blower protection, punishes state officials who fail to report corruption cases, and tries to prevent conflicts of interests. Amendments to the anti-corruption law were signed on December 7, 2009 increasing punishments for corruption, instituting mandatory asset forfeitures, broadening the definition of corruption crimes to include fraud committed by government officials, and criminalizing the acceptance of a bribe on behalf of a third party. The law also extended the definition of government official to managers of companies in which the government holds more than a 35% stake.

The Ministry of Interior, Financial Police, Disciplinary State Service Commission, and Committee for National Security (KNB) are responsible for combating corruption. However, questions of jurisdiction and competition between the Financial Police and KNB have occurred recently.

Transparency International (TI) maintains a national chapter in Kazakhstan. Kazakhstan's rating in TI's annual Corruption Perceptions Index is currently 2.8, placing Kazakhstan at 133 out of 176 countries rated -- a relatively weak score but the best for any country in Central Asia. TI experts have pointed out that corruption is particularly prevalent in the judiciary, police, customs, land registration, licensing, and construction projects. The government has signed on to the Extractive Industries Transparency Initiative (EITI) and is working to complete the validation process.

U.S. firms have cited corruption as a significant obstacle to investment. Law enforcement agencies occasionally have pressured foreign investors who are perceived to be uncooperative with the government, a practice that is made possible by the fact that many errors or omissions that would constitute routine civil violations in OECD countries are treated as criminal cases in Kazakhstan. The government and local business entities are widely aware of the legal restrictions placed on business abroad, such as the Foreign Corrupt Practices Act and the UK Bribery Act.

BILATERAL INVESTMENT AGREEMENTS

The United States-Kazakhstan Bilateral Investment Treaty came into force in 1994. In 1992, the United States and Kazakhstan signed an Investment Incentive Agreement.

In 1996, the Treaty on the Avoidance of Double Taxation between the United States and Kazakhstan came into force. Since independence, Kazakhstan has signed treaties on the avoidance of double taxation with 44 countries.

Kazakhstan has bilateral protection investment agreements with 47 countries, including Great Britain, Germany, Italy, France, Russia, South Korea, Iran, China, Turkey, and Vietnam. 30 of these 47 agreements have been ratified. In 2012, Kazakhstan signed investment agreements with Macedonia and Afghanistan. Some foreign investors charge that Kazakhstani tax authorities are very reluctant to refer double taxation questions to appropriate bi-national resolution bodies.

OPIC AND OTHER INVESTMENT INSURANCE PROGRAMS

The Overseas Private Investment Corporation (OPIC) has been active in Kazakhstan since 1994. OPIC is seeking commercially viable projects in Kazakhstan's private sector, and offers a full range of investment insurance and debt/equity stakes.

Kazakhstan is a member of the Multilateral Investment Guarantee Agency (MIGA), which is part of the World Bank Group that provides political risk insurance for foreign investments in developing countries.

LABOR

Kazakhstan has an educated workforce, although the proportion of highly technically competent workers is fairly small. Demand for skilled labor generally exceeds local supply. Technical skills, management expertise, and marketing skills are all in short supply. Many large investors rely on foreign workers and engineers to fill the void.

The Kazakhstani government has made it a priority to ensure that Kazakhstani citizens are well represented in foreign enterprise workforces. In 2009, the government instituted a comprehensive policy for local content, particularly for companies in the extractive industries (see Openness to, and restrictions upon, Foreign Investment and 5. Performance Requirements and Incentives). It is particularly keen to see Kazakhstanis hired into the managerial and executive ranks of foreign enterprises. Local content regulations require a minimum of 1% of a project budget be earmarked for training programs and workforce development, including overseas assignments with the lead operator. Employers' reliance on foreign labor in the face of poverty in rural Kazakhstan has become a political issue in recent years. In 2012, the minimum wage was $116.26 per month, and the minimum pension was $116.6 per month. By government estimates, the unemployment rate remained stable at just over 5% at the end of 2012.

A quota system for foreign employees and local content requirements creates an additional burden for employers. Several American and other foreign employees doing business in Kazakhstan have informed the U.S. Embassy that immigration authorities continue to scrutinize foreign work permits. U.S. companies are strongly advised to contact locally-based law and accounting firms and the U.S. Foreign Commercial Service in Almaty for updated information on work permits.

The Constitution and 2007 Labor Code guarantee basic workers' rights, including the right to organize and the right to strike. Workers can execute this right, if all arbitration measures defined by law are exhausted and solutions are not found. Decisions to strike must be taken in a meeting where at least half of workers are present.

Strikers must give five days advance notice to their employer and include a list of complaints as well as the date, the time and the place of strike. The court has the power to declare a strike illegal at the request of an employer or the General Prosecutor's office. Workers who participate in illegal strikes are subject to penalties. The Labor Code prohibits lockouts. The government is drafting a new law on Labor Unions.

Kazakhstan joined the International Labor Organization (ILO) in 1993. As of December 2012, Kazakhstan had ratified 19 ILO conventions, including those pertaining to minimum employment age, forced labor, discrimination in employment, equal remuneration, collective bargaining, the worst forms of child labor, and safety and health in construction. In 2011, Kazakhstan ratified Asbestos Convention 162.

FOREIGN TRADE ZONES/FREE TRADE ZONES

The 2011 Law on Special Economic Zones allows foreign companies to establish enterprises in special economic zones, simplifies procedures to attract foreign labor, and establishes a special customs zone regime not governed by Customs Union rules.

A system of tax preferences exists for foreign and domestic enterprises engaged in prescribed economic activities in Kazakhstan's nine Special Economic Zones (SEZ). The SEZs are located in the New Administrative Center in Astana, the Seaport of Aktau, the Alatau Information Technology Park (near Almaty), the Ontustik Cotton Center in south Kazakhstan, the international tourism zone "Borabay" (a resort area 300 kilometers from Astana), the Atyrau National Industrial Petrochemical Techno park, a metallurgical zone in the Karaganda region, a transport and logistics zone in Khorgos at the Kazakhstan-Chinese border, and a chemical zone in Pavlodar. Kazakhstan also plans to create a chemical industry SEZ in Taraz.

Summary Of Investments As Of 2012: As of June 30, 2012, Kazakhstan has received $171.9 billion of foreign direct investment since independence: 41.5% in business consulting and geological exploration, 12.9% in the financial sector, and approximately 14% in the extractive industries. U.S. firms have consistently ranked as some of Kazakhstan's largest foreign investors having invested $4.1 billion in the extractive sector. This includes large investments in Kazakhstan's petroleum sector by Chevron, ExxonMobil, and ConocoPhillips.

From 1993 to October 2012, Tengizchevroil, in which Chevron holds a 50% stake and ExxonMobil a 25% stake, contributed approximately $72.3 billion to Kazakhstani entities through purchases of Kazakhstani goods and services, tariffs and fees paid to state-owned companies, profit distributions to Kazakhstani shareholders, taxes and royalties paid to the government, and the salaries of employees.

Other foreign investors in the petroleum sector include the Chinese National Petroleum Corporation (CNPC), Shell, BG Group, Total, Agip, Lukoil, Eni, and Inpex. Other major U.S. investors in the broader economy include JP Morgan Chase&Co (over $300 million in business services), Marriott International (around $170 million in construction), and General Electric Transportation ($78 million in a locomotive facility). Non-U.S. major foreign investors include ArcelorMittal and BAE Systems.

FOREIGN DIRECT INVESTMENT STATISTICS

Table 1. Annual Gross Foreign Direct Investment Flows by Countries-Major Investors (Millions of Dollars; nominal)

	1993-2010	*2011*	*2012 (9 months)*	*Total*
USA	38,060.7	1,793.3	479.5	42,514.1
Netherlands	48,915.6	8,137.3	6,639.4	69,439.1
UK	17,963.9	799.2	340.8	20,124.7
Italy	9,511.7	455.2	-91.1	10, 448.1
France	13,240.9	1,545.3	839.3	17,158.7
Switzerland	7,349.8	443.8	411.9	8,683.2
Germany	1,175.5	125.7	362.6	1,855.3
South Korea	5,624.6	348.5	361.0	6,633.8
China	7,737.1	1,168.6	1,835.6	11,628.8
Canada	7,573.6	575.7	1,060.3	9,625.5
Russia	8,905.1	1,009.8	14.5	10,858.7
Japan	5,906.8	622.0	363.0	7,506.3
Turkey	2,771.7	123.3	137.6	3,122.8
British Virgin Islands	12,513.3	678.1	376.5	14,253.3
Others	36,500.3	2,983.3	3,894.0	46,727.7
TOTAL	**223,751.0**	**20,809.0**	**17,025.0**	**280,620.0**

Source: National Bank of Kazakhstan (the stock data is valued at market cost).

Table 2. Annual Gross Foreign Direct Investment Flows by Industries (Millions of U.S. Dollars; nominal)

	1993-2010	*2011*	*2012 (9 months)*	*Total*
agriculture, hunting and forestry	142.5	7.4	15.1	171.0
mining and quarrying	73,708.8	4,035.9	2,925.9	85,684.9
including, but not limited to extraction of crude petroleum and natural gas	65,130.3	2,208.6	1,519.8	72,644.7
manufacturing	21,311.5	2,855.4	1,619.1	27,836.2
electricity gas and air conditioning	573.5	116.1	154.5	914.0
water supply, sewage and waste management and remediation activities	0.4	9.3	-0.4	9.5
construction	3,786.9	414.8	899.7	5,523.8
wholesale and retail trade, repair of motor vehicles, motorcycles and personal and household goods	13,461.7	1,556.2	1,448.3	16,735.3

Table 2. (Continued)

	1993-2010	*2011*	*2012 (9 months)*	*Total*
food and accommodation services	576.3	27.1	27.7	659.6
transport& storage	2,365.6	208.0	282.4	2,921.6
information &communication	1,301.8	228.1	1,927.2	3,814.2
financial and insurance activity	13,104.8	407.6	1,169.5	15,209.7
real estate activities	1,337.8	165.4	69.3	1,705.0
professional, scientific & technical activities	85, 576.8	10,555.5	6,365.3	112,220.6
including but not limited to geological exploration and prospecting activities	80,109.1	8,821.8	4,985.0	102,316.7
education, health and social work services; arts, entertainment and recreation	383.3	16.8	11.5	426.7
Administration and support services	299.9	107.0	26.0	520.1
other	5,819.5	98.4	83.5	6,268.5
TOTAL	*223,751.0*	*20,809.0*	*17,025.0*	*280,620.0*

Source: National Bank of Kazakhstan.

Table 3. FDI as Percentage oF GDP (FLOW)

2010	2011	2012(9 months)
13%	11.4%	12.8%

Source: National Bank of Kazakhstan.

Table 4. Foreign Direct Investment (Stock) in Kazakhstan by Major Investors and Industries as of September 30, 2012 (Millions of U.S. dollars)

Direct Investment TOTAL	105, 804.0
AGRICULTURE, HUNTING AND FORESTRY	34.7
Including, but not limited to Netherlands	21.2
MINING AND QUARRYING	17,733.1
Including, but not limited to USA	2,495.8
Netherlands	5,994.0
China	3,383.5
Great Britain	570.9
Canada	1,687.0
MANUFACTURING	11,870.7
including, but not limited to Netherlands	9,147.0
Switzerland	1,621.0

Direct Investment TOTAL	105, 804.0
Great Britain	363.3
ELECTRICITY, GAS AND AIR CONDITIONING	698.8
Including, but not limited to British Virgin Islands	180.7
Netherlands	399.1
WATER SUPPLY, SEWERAGE & WASTE MANAGEMENT REMEDIATION ACTIVITIES	11.9
Including, but not limited to Netherlands	8.3
CONSTRUCTION	1,479.3
Including, but not limited to China	711.3
Netherlands	354.0
Turkey	23.3
Russia	111.9
WHOLESALE AND RETAIL TRADE, REPAIR OF MOTOR VEHICLES, AND PERSONAL AND HOUSEHOLD GOODS	3,814.8
Including, but not limited to Netherlands	964.5
Russia	631.6
Arab Emirates	832.4
ACCOMODATION AND FOOD SERVICES	191.1
Including, but not limited to Russia	2.7
Netherlands	108.5
TRANSPORT AND STORAGE	350.2
Including, but not limited to USA	70.5
Netherlands	58.1
INFORMATION AND COMMUNICATION	1,210
Netherlands	740.9
Cyprus	427.4
FINANCIAL AND INSURANCE ACTIVITY	5,367.7
Including, but not limited to Austria	1,471.0
Netherlands	249.5
Great Britain	349.2
USA	308.5
Russia	795.7
China	201.5
PROFESSIONAL, SCIENTIFIC & TECHNICAL ACTIVITIES	60,077.4
Including, but not limited to Netherlands	25,500.8
USA	12,263.5
France	7,994.9
Japan	3,606.2
Great Britain	261.6

Source: National Bank of Kazakhstan (the stock data is valued at market cost).

Table 5. FDI (stock) as Percentage of GDP

As of September 30, 2012	80.1%

Table 6. Kazakhstani Direct Investment Outflows (Millions of U.S. dollars, nominal)

Country of Destination	2004-2011	2012(9 months)	Total
Netherlands	36,499.9	1,254.8	37,754.7
Great Britain	5,815.7	-37.1	5,778.6
Russia	3,354.6	74.8	3,429.4
Virgin Islands	1,942.4	-74.4	1,868.0
Turkey	1,377.5	-14.0	1,363.6
Switzerland	1,299,9	17.9	1,317.8
USA	1,265.0	0.5	1,265.5
Cyprus	933.3	0.8	934.2
Kyrgyzstan	829.2	-5.5	823.6
Ukraine	710.0	8.8	718.7
Germany	479.6	1.0	480.6
China	343.6	21.2	364.8
Arab Emirates	220.5	344.2	564.7
Other Countries	2,248.0	247.1	2,495.0
TOTAL	57,319.0	1,840.0	59,159.0

Source: National Bank of Kazakhstan.

INDEX

A

B

C

D

F

G

H

K

L

M

Q

R

S

T

U

V

W